HER STORY

IS

My Story

HER TRUTH, MY HEALING

MICHELLE DOWLEYNE AND 16 COURAGEOUS Co-AUTHORS

Library of Congress Cataloging-in-Publication Data

Scripture quotations are taken from the Holy Bible, New Living Translation (NIV), copyright © 1996, 2004, 2007, 2013, 2015 by Tyndale House Foundation.

Editing: SynergyEd Consulting/ synergyedconsulting.com
Graphics & Cover Design: Greenlight Creations Graphics Designs glightcreations.com/ glightcreations@gmail.com

sherp *publishing*

Published by: SHERO Publishing
getpublished@sheropublishing.com

S H E R O P U B L I S H I N G . C O M

W W W . M I C H E L L E D O W L E Y N E . C O M

Table of Contents

HER Story:

Dedication

This book is dedicated to my children, who have been through all of life's up and downs with me. You had no choice, in many of the circumstances you were in, but at no time did you complain. You remained humble, obedient, and never questioned my choices. There were days that I could not show you the love that you deserved because I wasn't whole. So today, as I stand changed, I say, *I love you infinity*.

To my husband, whom God sent into my life at the right time, for He knows best. I thank you for never wavering your love for me. You did not sign up for the sleepless nights, mood shifts, days on top of days of depression, but at no time have you left me alone. I thank you for allowing me to be me and share my journey of transformation with the world. The word says when he who finds a wife, finds a good thing, but I honestly was the one who found *a good man*.

To the SHERO Publishing staff; the amazing Book Coaches that worked with our Co-Author group weekly to support our book project, Coach Kimberly Perry Sanderlin and Marketing Director Camilla Moore. Thank you to CEO Erica Perry Green and the entire SHERO Publishing Team for all your help, collaboration and support to make this project a reality.

To the Co-Authors, my new family: Thank You, Thank You, and Thank You again for sharing your vulnerability to the world to allow others to heal. The planning sessions we shared bought healing to all our lives in ways we may have never experienced, had we not been placed together. I pray that as you continue to share your story, that multiple people will be blessed and began a healing process for themselves. May you know that you are exactly where God wants you to be for Him to use you. Walk into your season and be blessed with all that He has in store for you.

Introduction

The vision for this book was clear. Looking back over my life, I have had many trials and tribulations, but I survived. There were days that I felt so alone and felt that no one would understand me. I thought that no one else could be going through the horrible things that I was going through. I was embarrassed and ashamed of my life. Then, my spirit spoke to me, "*Other women are dealing with the same issues, and some have no support group. Bring the healing to them.*" Those words activated my mission and this compilation, **Her Story Is My Story– Her Truth, My Healing**. My vision is also for men to understand women who are secretly hurting. I want men to use this book as a resource to support their mothers, wives, sisters and daughters.

This compilation will help to transform *fears to faith*, *unhappiness to hope,* and *tears to joy*! Readers will be empowered to release the weight of the world and drop the baggage that people have held on to for far too long. My hope is that these powerful 17 stories will help readers to know that they are NOT alone. I pray that as they read from these courageous women, they will feel that, *Her Story is My Story* and *Her Truth is My Healing.*

~*Author Michelle Dowleyne*

www.michelledowleyne.com

HER STORY IS MY STORY

HER TRUTH,
MY HEALING

PRESENTING OUR CO-AUTHORS

Author Amber Clark

Amber Clark

Amber A. Clark was born in Atlanta, Georgia and currently resides in Atlanta. She is a retired Army veteran, a member of the Head Start Policy Council, and a parent volunteer. Amber believes that we can change the world, one person at a time through engagement, encouragement, and love. She wants to advocate for the speechless children and minorities living in poverty conditions. Her educational background includes an Associate degree in Liberal Arts from Central Texas College, a B.S in Psychology from the University of Maryland and a certification in Human Resource Management. However, her biggest accomplishment is being a mother to her two daughters, Tiara and Mia. She loves spending time with family, traveling, and learning about history.

In reading her chapter, she hopes that others can use her experience to overcome situations that seem dark and challenging. Amber believes that there is a bigger picture to every small challenge, and she continues to push through even in the darkest times. She hopes that this writing platform that God has given her can spread love and hope to others. Amber reminds us that Philippians 4:13 states: *I can do all things through him who strengthens me.* She encourages us to-**Say it, Believe it, and Do it.**

The Rising Phoenix

I was that wounded, broken, and battered bird. Four years ago, you couldn't tell me I would be reborn, stronger, and shining like a rising phoenix; but yes, I have risen. Greek folklore describes the phoenix as a bird that is reborn and rises from its ashes, stronger, better, and renewed. One evening in March 2020, at about 9:45 p.m., I was laying in the bed talking to my girlfriend from work and waiting on *the call*. We were just joking and laughing to distract my mind from what my body was already exhibiting. About ten minutes later, I received *the call* that would change my world forever. "Ms. Clark, Is this Miss Clark? I have your results and you have tested positive for the coronavirus." I paused just long enough to let the words process through my mind, but then I was interrupted with- "You will receive a call from the nurse and the health department in a few days." I was confused and scared.

Now that it was confirmed that I was affected, I now had to make sure I did not contaminate anyone else, including my children. I clicked back over to my friend, and she asked what the results of my test were. Once I informed her of the diagnosis, her laugh turned into concern for my welfare as well as hers. My mind began racing with a million questions, "Where did I go that I could have caught it? Did my kids have it? Will I die? What will my job say? Did I affect my colleagues?" I thought hearing that my test was positive was hard, but the hard part was just beginning.

I quarantined myself to my room and called my mother to ask her to come wipe everything down in my home, except my room and bathroom, because I did not want to infect her or my children. My mother told my children the news and explained to them that

"Mommy, cannot be around you and you cannot go into her room or use her bathroom. The hardest thing to hear was my five-year-old say, "Mommy is sick and I'm sad. I don't want her to die." I just cried silently, because just as sad and scared as they were, so was I.

Every day the media was reporting another death in isolation from this coronavirus. I prayed, "Lord please help me to fight this and survive. I can't leave my children or mother." For the first two days, I only experienced heaviness on my chest, dry throat, lack of appetite, and extreme weakness. But on day three, I started to fight to live. I was dozing off quickly and frequently. I would wake completely drained. My perspiration soiled through my clothes and bedsheet. I would try to walk, but my body ached so badly that I was shaking like a fragile 90-year-old woman and I was only in my 30's!

I was receiving calls constantly from my doctors, the health department, and Veteran Affairs about the worsening changes that were occurring in my body. I was getting more scared by the day because the most frightening fact was, there wasn't a treatment that could cure this. There was no medicine that would help this coronavirus leave my body quickly. I was filled with fear as the nurse told me, "We are sending you an inhaler, Supatimin, and a decongestant medication. That's all we can do because you must let it run its course." I was told to stay hydrated and to rest, but still not a word of a definite cure. By the fifth day, I wasn't only physically struggling, I was mentally fighting, as well. I could hear my daughters talking and I recognized the fear and distress in their voices. I knew my illness placed a tremendous burden on my oldest daughter. Now, she had to attend school, watch her younger sister, clean the house, wash the dishes, and try to cook for herself and her sibling. My baby was sleeping and depressed and there wasn't anything I could do. I felt like a failure, as a mother, because I thought somehow my catching the coronavirus was my fault and, in all honesty, I didn't know what the outcome would be.

By week two, I was so weak that I couldn't even bathe myself. Everything hurt and I was so uncomfortable and miserable. I was crying because the coronavirus death toll was increasing and my children were suffering. I couldn't even talk to my babies and they were in the same house as me! My mother had to stop coming by to check on us because she was suffering from her own underlying ailment and the fear of me infecting her was overwhelming. It was hard to think of. However, my brother came every day; masked and ready to help me. It was during my first month of having the coronavirus that I lost my sense of taste and smell. I remember having a quick urge to go to the bathroom to spit out phlegm. My body was so sore and weak that I was dragging and trembling as I walked across the room to the bathroom. As I attempted to get to the toilet, I started choking and wheezing from the phlegm that was lodged in my chest and throat. I was losing consciousness! I thought, "This is it; I will die in this bathroom and no one will even know because I am isolated from everyone. They will find my dead body in here, too late." But God knew that I was in danger. I was struggling to breathe, and I was getting ready to hit the floor when my brother entered my room.

When I gained the strength to look up, my brother was there. As we locked eyes, he saw the fear and heard me choking on my own phlegm. My brother started screaming at me; he was trying to get me to breathe while yelling at my daughter to call 911! He immediately ran and got my inhaler, with the steroids in it, to open my lungs. As he was pumping the medication into me, I saw nothing but fear in his eyes. After that scare, I realized then, that I couldn't give in and give up. I needed my family just as much as they needed me. So, I began to eat even though I couldn't taste anything. My body needed the fuel. I constantly drank liquids.

During this time, I had multiple coworkers, friends, and family that had food delivered to me and my family, so I was loaded with soup and hot tea. Slowly but steadily, I started to regain my strength. I was now determined to fight to live. I started getting out of my bed and walking from the bed to the bathroom door. Each day, my walk grew stronger. Just like the *Phoenix*, I had risen from the ashes; stronger and better! I started to see the positive in this Covid moment. I needed to suffer to appreciate the blessings that I had all this time. You see, God had started me on this journey at the age of three, when I survived being a burn victim. During that time, I suffered third-degree burns and spent months in recovery. As a young child, something that should have killed me prepared me to be the *Phoenix* I was meant to be. Now, as an adult, I used that preparation as I fought against the attack on my body.

I recovered within four months from the coronavirus. Throughout my ordeal, my relationship with God and my daughters grew stronger. Through my sickness and fighting for my life, God provided total restoration and even increase! In the midst of a pandemic, I was empowered. I became a homeowner, an author, and I received a promotion. I died metaphorically, but I rose from my tears, pain, and struggle to soar as a strong, divine, and powerful ***Phoenix***!

How Her Story Relates to My Story:

_____

_____

_____

_____

_____

_____

_____

_____

_____

_____

_____

_____

How Her Story Relates to My Story:

_____

_____

_____

_____

_____

_____

_____

_____

_____

_____

_____

_____

Author Demaryl Roberts-Singleton

Demaryl Roberts-Singleton

Demaryl D. Singleton was born in Cleveland, Ohio, and she now resides in Bryans Road, Maryland. She enjoys spending time with her family, friends and traveling abroad. Demaryl has been married to Cedric M. Singleton for 27 years. She has two adult children: Jamaii C. Singleton and Walter B. Whitsett II, from a previous marriage.

In 1970. At the age of seven, Demaryl was removed from her parent's home by the Ohio Department of Social Services. Demaryl learned that she had lived with a foster family for the first seven years of her life. Demaryl was physically and emotionally abused after being placed with her real family. She became a teenage mother. Her life was not easy growing up in Cleveland, but God was there every step of the way through all her ups and downs. During this chapter of her life, Demaryl believes it is essential for her to share her experience with the world and let young adults living in an abusive situation and poverty know there is hope. She shares that staying inspired each day was not easy, but it was essential for keeping her inner fire lit and moving towards her personal and professional goals.

Today, Demaryl Singleton has thirty-seven years of dedicated Federal Civil Service. She is the Program Manager of the Department of Defense Teleport System. She leads this $3.1B program and is responsible for the design, development, system engineering, acquisition testing, integration, implementation, and life cycle management of the Teleport System. Through a multi-generational, evolutionary development approach, Demaryl is responsible for integrating and implementing satellite terminals and the ground station baseband equipment to enable secured voice, data, and video communications to deployed warfighters: thus, enhancing situational awareness and information superiority globally.

Demaryl Singleton holds a B.S. in Management from Park University and a master's degree in Procurement and Acquisition Management, and a Master's in Business Administration (MBA) with an emphasis in Information Technology Management from Webster University. While working for the Department of Defense, Demaryl obtained her Defense Acquisition Workforce Improvement Act (DAWIA) Level III Certification in Contracting, Information Technology Management, and Program Management from the Defense Acquisition University (DAU). She is a member of the Defense Acquisition Corps, American Society of Military Comptrollers Association, Defense Acquisition University Voting Member, National Council of Negro Women Incorporated, Order of the Eastern Star (OES), Queen of Sheba Chapter #2-Washington, DC and Ancient Egyptian Arabic Order Nobles Mystic Shrine North and South and its Jurisdictions Inc. (A.E.A.O.N.M.S), Misr Court #193.

Demaryl Singleton holds numerous awards that include: The Commanders Award for Civilian Service Deployment, Civilian of the Year Air Force Academy (1992), and The Navy's Civilian Meritorious Award (1998).

Just a Colored Girl from Cleveland Who "Suffered and Succeeded"

I decided to tell my story, hoping to inspire troubled teenagers and young adult women globally. My sisters, there is hope at the end of the tunnel. My life was not easy growing up in Cleveland, but God was there every step of the way, through all my ups and downs. God has traveled beside me and protected me throughout my life's journey, through both the difficult and the good times. However, no matter the situation, I have always had an emotional attitude of gratitude. No matter what was happening in my life, having faith and directing my energy helped me stay centered and grounded. My "why" is the action that came from within, and my fulfillment is to *finally* tell my story.

My journey began in the early 60s. I learned that shortly after I was born, my mother was raped. As a result of the traumatic experience, she suffered a nervous breakdown. The State of Ohio removed all four of her children and put us in foster homes. My three siblings were sent to the same foster home and were raised together. For some reason, perhaps because I was so young, I was sent to a separate foster home. Soon, my three siblings were returned home. I was the only one that remained in a foster home for seven years.

For seven years, I experienced a good childhood; raised by the Johnsons, a Christian family that showed me love. Then came that dreadful day of removal in 1970. At the age of seven, I was ripped from my *parents'* home by the Cuyahoga Department of Social Services. It was then that I learned the Johnsons were my *foster* family and that I had been in and out of several foster homes during the first two months of my life. On many occasions, I would call my foster momma and beg her to come and get me. Unfortunately, my foster mom died from a massive heart attack, four months after the social service department removed me from her home. I cried so many tears for years; thus, I became very shy, timid, afraid to talk to people, and was in a state of shock. I lost track of my foster family, and my only regret today is that I don't have any contact with my foster family.

In 1970, I was returned to my birth mother. Growing up with my real family was like living a tragedy. The next ten years of my life were hell. My real mom physically and emotionally abused me and all her children. She beat us with extension cords and cursed at us repeatedly. My sister and I would run away from home after getting beat with extension cords. We would stay with strangers or relatives for a couple of days at a time. We didn't get gifts and would tell lies to our friends during the Christmas season, so we wouldn't be embarrassed about not getting toys and new clothes. My childhood till the age of seven had been normal; I grew up in a loving home. I can't remember ever getting a spanking from my foster parents. Having experienced a normal childhood, made the life I was now living even harder.

For the first time, I was experiencing true poverty. We were on welfare, and we moved from house to house, all over Cleveland. Being severely impoverished, we often faced food shortages. In the winter, we often didn't have hats, gloves, or boots and we had to walk several miles to school. My mother never told us that she loved us; there was no mention of love in our house. She would use horrific language and was always threatening to beat us. My mom was angry because my dad left her, living in poverty with seven kids. At the age of ten, I met my dad for the first time and learned that he had fathered so many kids.

Growing up in Cleveland was tough, and I was exposed to drugs, alcohol, and crime at a young age. On May 8, 1976, at the age of twelve, our family was highlighted on the Cleveland Plain Dealer's front page, and the article was titled, "End of a Dream: Rent Ceiling Prevents Mother of 7 Children from Finding Decent Housing". My mother had us looking like the Little Rascals in the article. I was teased and humiliated by our friends due to our poor living conditions. Mysteriously, one of our homes caught on fire, and I always believed that my mom intentionally set it on fire for sympathy. I remember that one of the few good times for my siblings and me was going to Hiram House Camp for two weeks every summer.

At the age of fourteen, I met my first real boyfriend and fell in love and we dated throughout high school. At the age of seventeen, I unintentionally got pregnant. I hid the pregnancy almost nine months. During my pregnancy, I took the welfare medical card and went to all my scheduled doctor appointments without anybody knowing that I was pregnant. I gave birth on April 25, 1981, on my abusive mother's birthday. She became a grandmother on her birthday, and she was excited and happy for me until that dreadful day that I requested welfare assistance for my son's birth. We got into a dispute; she physically abused me then chased me down the street with a gun, threatening to shoot me with my two-month-old baby in my arms! I left home with nothing and never looked back. I was homeless with my baby boy until my future husband's sister provided a place to stay until we got married on September 10, 1981, and we moved into my in-laws' home until we got our apartment. My struggle didn't change as a result of marriage. My husband and I were barely making it, and I was working two jobs and going to school. My husband was protected by his parents and could do no wrong in their Christian eyes, especially since I came from the rough side of town and didn't have a stable, loving home. During that time, my husband's family had a reputation of being a well-to-do, honorable Christian family. His parents didn't know that I helped him finish high school by writing his papers and completing his homework assignments because he was too busy getting high and drinking. After high school, he couldn't hold a job due to his drug use, drinking, and running Cleveland's streets with his friends. His parents had no clue that I had to hold down a job while attending school and caring for a newborn baby. In 1982, I forced my husband to study for the Armed Services Vocational Aptitude Battery, and he passed the test for the Air Force, and went into the service on the delayed entry program in 1983.

The first significant change toward happiness within my adult life happened in 1983 when my son, my husband's best friend's pregnant wife, and I left Cleveland on a Greyhound bus headed to Plattsburgh Air Force Base, in New York. Our husbands joined the Air Force, and they happened to get stationed together, and Plattsburgh was our first base. I landed my first government position at the Airmen's Club, serving pizza, subs, and beer. At times, I was serving alcoholic drinks when the bartenders didn't show up to work. Funny thing, I was clueless when making alcoholic drinks! However, I was making big money in tips.

Tragically in 1984, my oldest sister passed away from viral meningitis, at the age of 24. Her death was devastating and senseless. She had been sick, but no one took her seriously. People made fun of her, including our family members; they minimized her condition until it was too late. She became very sick and passed away.

In September 1984, I took my first international flight, headed to Frankfurt, Germany, and we were stationed at Hahn Air Force Base. During that same year, I became a civil servant as a GS-02. Life was good, and I truly enjoyed living and traveling abroad.

In 1985, I traveled to the US on emergency leave to attend my sister-in-law's funeral in Harlem. We missed the funeral, and I learned that people don't drive in New York City. After the repast, we traveled to Cordele, Georgia, the home of my husband's parents. I couldn't understand why my husband's father didn't attend his own daughter's funeral in New York. At that time, I suggested to my husband that we meet his two sisters, he asked his mom and dad for the addresses. His parents barred us from seeing his sisters. Of course, I thought that was strange as hell. We had traveled all the way from Germany, and I had never met his sisters. I said to my husband, "We are adults, so get ready, because we will see them anyway." I met both sisters, and the youngest sister said to me that she hated her dad because, as a little girl, he raped her repeatedly throughout her teenage years. The oldest sister said that the family believed that their dad had killed their mom after the youngest child's birth. The youngest child was the sister who had just confided in me that she had been raped by her father. To this day, I can still hear her voice telling me what her dad did to her, and her stepmom covered up her husband's crime. I learned so much about this so-called Christian family and why all my husband's siblings left Cleveland; they left because they hated their parents.

In 1988, we left Germany and moved to Colorado Springs, Colorado, and by that time, the marriage was in trouble. My spouse was cheating and having issues with his dad being accused by his sister to be a sexual pedophile and rapist. We separated and then divorced on October 31, 1990, and the judge awarded me custody of my son. My son and I moved into a place near the Air Force Academy. My life drastically changed while living in Colorado Springs; I was a single mom raising my son. During that period, I became an African Dancer, and my stage name was Jamaii, in our group, UMOJA. We performed traditional African dancing throughout Colorado and Texas at many charity events sponsored by the Masonic lodges, Greek sororities and fraternities, churches, and community organizations. One evening in 1990, while I was working my part-time job, my ten-year-old son was attacked and choked by a White South African man who told him he was going to "kick his ass to the moon". This man was my neighbor, who was in the United States through the smuggling of diamonds. I secured a restraining order against the attacker. He was fired as a professor from the University of Colorado Springs because I provided documentation to the University of the crime he committed against my son. As a single parent, I had to fight for more than two years to make the legal system work for us. I definitely was no longer that timid, shy, afraid-to-speak-to-people personality from my childhood. Sparked by the abuse to my son, I was now, the very vocal and persistent advocate for justice. I wrote the following local and national agencies: the FBI, Immigration and Naturalization, the NAACP, and the Urban League. He violated the restraining order several times, and he continued to harass my son and me. I continued to contact the District Attorney's Office in Colorado almost daily until we finally went to court, and he lost. After he lost the case, he once again violated the restraining order and was sent to jail; tried and convicted of a misdemeanor. My case just missed the cut-off date to have been processed under the hate crime bill that was signed by President William Clinton. The White South African man would have been charged as a felon under the Hate Crime Act.

My life changed in 1993; I remarried, and my daughter was born the following year. My daughter Jamaii, was named after my stage name when I was a dancer in UMOJA. All was going well. Then, my husband, who was an Officer in the Military, decided to leave the Army, after six years of active duty, to begin working in Corporate America. Being used to the stability and benefits of the military, I was upset and afraid of being poor and the possible change in lifestyle. We moved from Colorado to Texas with a four-month-old baby. This move was the true acceleration of my professional career. I started working for the Navy in 1994, followed by employment with General Services Administration, Navy, Air Force, Department of Defense, Combined Federal Campaign, and the Army. My husband and I relocated to several locations throughout the United States. Despite all my mom's physical and emotional abuse of me during my childhood, I did forgive her and we built a good relationship. I understood why she did what she did. In 2006, my mom lost her battle with Aplastic Anemia, and my dad passed in December of that year from diabetes, heart, and kidney disease. My youngest sister passed away in 2012 from pneumonia.

Almost immediately after coming into this world, I became a foster child, later was stripped from my loving foster parents, then physically and emotionally abused by my birth mother that I had not known, lived in poverty, and without expressions of love. Yet, through God, I survived, through the grace of God I prospered! Education and leaving Cleveland, Ohio were the keys to my success. I have always had God, good intentions, inspired dreams, and energy throughout every stage of my life. I am so grateful for the achievements that I have received. Community service and being a loving person have always been my focus and my forte'. Throughout my journey, I have been blessed to have traveled globally for business and personal vacations. I have traveled to 41 of the 50 states and 39 countries. I deployed as a civil servant with the Department of the Army for fourteen months to Kuwait in 2013. Today I have a Bachelor of Science in Management, Master's in Art, Procurement and Acquisition Management, and an MBA with a Concentration in Information Technology Management. I began my career with the Department of Defense at the bottom of the pay scale and as a food service worker. Today, I am in a senior role in the Department of Defense, leading a major acquisition program valued at $3.1 billion. Today, I am looking to retire after thirty-seven years in the Department of Defense and seeking employment by taking my education and skills learned over the years into the private sector. The blessing is the fact that I have unique talents, experience, and education.

During this current chapter of my life, it is essential for me that I share my story with the world and let young adults, living in poverty, know there is hope. Staying inspired each day is not easy, but it's essential for keeping your inner fire lit and moving towards your goals. Always believe in yourself and surround yourself with wisdom and positive people. The most challenging thing for me is the decision to act; the rest is merely tenacity. I am grateful for each day, everything that I have received in life, and most importantly, I treasure the family and friendships gained throughout my travels. I am so grateful for the things that are still coming, like new possibilities, opportunities, and life connections. Whatever I focus on, I tend to attract my blessings from that source. I have learned that whatever I do or dream of in life, it all begins with boldness and having the power to do it. Success for me is having the energy to receive happiness through God in order to get what I want. This testimony gave my life meaning, a sense of purpose, and the fuel to tell this story of a colored girl from Cleveland who struggled and succeeded

How Her Story Relates to My Story:

_____

_____

_____

_____

_____

_____

_____

_____

_____

_____

_____

_____

How Her Story Relates to My Story:

_____

_____

_____

_____

_____

_____

_____

_____

_____

_____

_____

_____

Author Denise Rankin

Denise Rankin

Denise Rankin is a woman who has overcome everything meant to steal her life and destroy her spirit! Raised in the Flint, Michigan, life wasn't easy, but through all her struggles, Denise has persevered. After losing her son, in a police shooting, Denise decided to relocate her family to Sachse, Texas for a fresh start, away from all the hurt, pain, and great loss that they suffered in Flint.

With an entrepreneurial spirit, Denise launched her own cosmetics business, while working in hospitality services. She now serves as an Executive Director for Einnaf Cosmetics, mentoring and coaching other women entrepreneurs. Denise has a passion to help women push through those things that they faced, particularly women who have faced incarceration and mothers who have lost children to police shootings.

Denise hopes that her journey and the messages within her chapter, will bless others and let them know that overcoming is possible. Denise strives to show her children that life after great tragedy is possible. She desires to leave a legacy of being a wonderful mother and God-fearing woman who makes an impact on the lives of others. Denise knows that Jesus gives her the strength to withstand it all.

Contact information:
Website: lavishinglips.com
Email: rankin_denise@yahoo.com
Facebook: www.facebook.com/DeniseRankin
Instagram: Denise.Rankin12

Dope Game~ Trapped in My Mind:
The Hood Won't Leave Me Alone

We all have dreams… My dreams included becoming a successful businesswoman who advocated for teens. I grew up in a family of six. As a teenager, I become pregnant with my first son and did not graduate from high school. I quickly had to teach myself how to survive and be an independent woman. So, I moved out at the age of eighteen into my own house. During this time, many men came and went… but I still strived to get closer to that original goal.

Thankfully, I was able to earn my GED with the help of a man who cared very much for me. He would stay at home with my son while I was in my classes. During this period, we became closer, and our relationship grew. Eventually, this man became the father of my second child. To support our growing family, I had numerous jobs. I even tried to get a modeling career off the ground but didn't have any support from my overly protective family. The men in my life weren't responsible enough to take care of me and my children. I always depended on myself to get the job and work and provide for my family, but bills began to pile up. Work wasn't enough. Frustration and despair drove me to try something different. I got involved with the number one killer: drugs. Mr. Cocaine himself. Thankfully, a raid early on in my addiction was all I needed to convince me that drugs were not the life for me. But it was right out of the frying pan and into the fire; for in my next move, I became involved with a new man who *sold* drugs. I ran into a dirty cop who framed me into a 10-year sentence with the feds!

Childhood

I am sitting on my bed with headphones on, turned up loud. My oldest sister is washing dishes. My younger sister and brother are running and screaming because our dad and mom are fighting. I am shaken by the sound of my father slapping and punching my mom and my mom screaming for him to stop. I grabbed my younger siblings and did my best to console them. As I rocked my young siblings, I couldn't help but think that a real man wouldn't hit a woman. I secretly can't wait for all of us to be old enough to be away from the violence.

My mother did not work; her life as a housewife is probably why she stayed in such a violent relationship. Every now and then she would take odd jobs, but my father would not allow her to keep the jobs long. To him, it was the man's job to work and the woman's job to be at home with the children. Years passed and my mother continued to be under my dad's thumb. Finally, as if out of the blue, she seemed to wake up from her fog; fed up with years and now more than a decade of abuse. The mother of four was finally fed up with my dad's constant gambling, clubbing, and cheating. I couldn't have been prouder of her when she finally decided to leave him.

As a teen growing up in turmoil, I always wanted to experience what other teens regularly enjoyed. Unlike my peers, I wasn't allowed to go on school trips to Cedar Point or Kings Island. I felt that my childhood was meaningless. Out of retaliation and anger, I began skipping school with other students- drinking and smoking weed at house parties. To get me back on track, my mother decided she would appeal to my interest in modeling and connect me with a modeling agency. Modeling captured my interest, and everything was fine up until the modeling agency's scheduled trip to New York. My family didn't allow me to go… and I was crushed! Modeling made me feel beautiful and important. Not able to model, I lost interest in high school; I just stopped going. I resented my mother for not allowing me to actualize my modeling career.

Adulthood

As I became an adult, I did not give up on my modeling career. I went to different modeling agencies… each one seemed to be more expensive than the next. I did not have the money it took to get make-up and headshots. At this point, I had three beautiful children and bills that had to take priority. When I was twenty-three years old, my parents separated after 20 plus years. Their separation was devastating to the family.

I had become accustomed to a certain lifestyle, so I continued to look towards the fast life to help finance my desires. I became involved with a younger man who was not responsible and couldn't care for me and my family. My brother was selling drugs and I became curious about following in his footsteps. He introduced me to a couple of fellas that helped me get my own thing off the ground. After a couple of months, I was easily bringing home five thousand dollars a week. I was addicted to what my new career afforded me: buying expensive clothes for family and friends, going to hair and nail salons, and shopping every week.

No matter how lucrative the drug game got for me, I always kept my 9-to-5. One day after a long day of work, I went out to a nightclub to party with my friends. Lots of drinking and dancing was going on, and I indulged in it ALL. I didn't get back home until 5 or 6 in the morning. I was so intoxicated that I couldn't even make it to the bedroom; I just passed out on the floor. After a while, I heard a knock at the door but couldn't muster the energy and control it took to get to the door. The person on the other side was persistent; they knocked for at least 5 minutes. I finally was able to get up and answer the door… only to find a female walking across the street. She glanced my way. Somehow, she knew there was a sell to be sold. Not one to shy away from a quick sell, I called the lady back over to the house. Boy, was that a bad move! The lady was an informant for the police. Four hours after selling to her, our home was raided. It was something like you see in the movies. About five officers came in and they were on a mission. The neighbors took my kids until my family was able to pick them up.

I always carried a Taurus 9-millimeter with cop-killer bullets for protection. They did not find drugs in the house. My boyfriend left a single crack cocaine rock in a Crazy Glue bottle in my kitchen. My gun was found on top of the refrigerator inside of my purse. The house was turned upside-down. My boyfriend and I were escorted to the city jail. I stayed for a couple of hours. We were given a court date and told when to appear. I took all charges because the house was rented in my name. Through it all, the love that I had for my children's father kept me from admitting to authorities that the crack they found was his.

On the morning of our court date, I had a nagging feeling that something bad was going to happen. The "goodbye" from my youngest son was weighted with a feeling of doom. My mother went to court with me. I remember picking out a pretty dress in hopes of impressing the judge. The prosecutor dropped the gun charge, which was a mandatory five years; they knew the judge was going to hang me. But being that I had never gotten into any trouble, he gave me 30 days in jail, 6 months on tether, and 5-years probation. I was able to successfully complete my sentence in 2 ½ years. I was convinced that I had learned my lesson. I got a job and life was getting on track. Everything was working out fine.

Then my life began to shift downhill once again. Taking my drug-dealing brother on errands soon got me caught back up into the drug game once again. Only this time, I was introduced to a drug dealer who loved to spend money on me... Again, I felt beautiful. I knew this man was wrong for me, but I continued to date him. I felt like "it's on him if he gets caught." I felt that I was invincible because I wasn't doing anything wrong. I guess if I'd been paying closer attention to felony law, I would have known better than to be dating him. At the time of dating, this drug dealer heard that my children's father and I had broken up but were on good enough terms to cohabit for the kids. My children's father had no idea that I was drawing closer to this other man. I began going out with the drug dealer to dinner, clubs, hotels, and on a few occasions, to his home. I was intrigued by the lifestyle that dating this man afforded me; I was now in over my head. During my visitation to his home, I met a couple of his friends. One day while with my best friend, she hit it off with one of his best friends. After a couple of dates, their relationship escalated. Two months later these men had to move and needed a place to stay because they didn't want to go back to Dot. The man who had been dating my friend offered to pay her phone bill, buy food, and let her drive his car. As a single mother, this offer was enticing and acceptable to my friend. Just as quickly as he moved in, we realized that it was a horrible idea. Why? We found out that he really wasn't into her. After providing him keys to her house, she discovered he was running drugs out of her home. He had to go!

Once he was gone, she still allowed my boyfriend to stay there because of our friendship. In hindsight, I feel that my best friend did it for more than our friendship; I think she got jealous because her relationship didn't turn out to be her *dream come true*. She saw how my boyfriend constantly wined and dined me and wanted that for herself. Soon after my boyfriend moved in with my best friend, I noticed the tides began to turn... I began calling my boyfriend's pager and got no response. I'd call my best friend- same thing! Thoughts came to mind because he always returned my calls. The best friend was having sex with my man!

I asked him the next day why he didn't answer his pager; his response was "I was asleep." I didn't believe that. I demanded that he move out if he wanted our relationship to continue... I would soon find that it was not the case. One day, I picked him up under the assumption that we would go to Blockbuster, order a pizza, and spend the evening at my sister's house, as usual. On the way to Blockbuster, he tells me "I'm going back home." What?! I explained to him that I had already made plans with my sister. For me, that was the icing on the cake! What was so important that he would rather be at my best friend's house?! I took him "home" and told him it was over.

A couple of weeks passed by and he'd gotten his own apartment and asked me to move in. While I seriously considered the offer, I knew it would hurt my family and my children's father. I also was still upset about what went down between him and my best friend. So, I got it in my mind to toy with him, out of spite. I told him "yes." I didn't take his key because the two times I went to the apartment; his friends were there. I asked him "why are they here?" He didn't reply. But I overheard them talking about staying in the apartment upstairs. This is not what I wanted. I knew it would be trouble if these men were anywhere close by, so I decided not to move in. I felt that he had lied to me. These men were drug-dealers, and I knew they would be running business out of the house. My brother hung out with the same men, so I had my confirmation that it was a bad idea.

My brother had a girlfriend who was introduced to him by our older sister. This girlfriend had already been put out of several houses due to her own drug addiction, however, she and my brother ended up staying at our father's house. Our father had to put them out on several occasions because they wouldn't pay rent and because they were selling drugs. My brother had several run-ins with the police, and the girlfriend was in deep trouble for cutting off a tether. In order for my brother to stay out of trouble with the law, his girlfriend became an informant for the Flint Police Department. At the time, I was not aware of their arrangement with the cops... but God did try to warn me in many ways. Too bad, I ignored the warning signs. When I would drop the girlfriend off, my mother would tell me "You need to go home to those babies." I told my mom that I would be back in a while, and still went to my brother and his girlfriend's spot.

After being at their house less than an hour, we heard a big boom at the door. It was the Flint Police Department raiding the house. No drugs were found on me- only $60 and a pager - which every cop feels is needed to sell drugs. A couple of guns and additional pagers were found. A dog was at the scene. The dog found drugs beside the living room sofa inside a gym bag; the drugs were inside a Ziplock that was inside another bag. I remember thinking how trained that animal had to be to find those drugs so quickly... I quickly wished that I had been trained enough to stay away from this life...

Everyone, including me, was taken into police custody for two days. My brother and I were released without any pending charges, but my boyfriend stayed in custody. I tried to get my car back because it was confiscated by the police. Without a lawyer, I went down to the police station to get my car. The car was not released to me because they felt I had drugs at the house that they missed because someone had informed them that I did. In order to proclaim my innocence, I let my sister get tricked into staying in the police department. I was escorted by the police officer through a secret way back to my house, with no warning to my family.

After the raid, the police officer called me into the kitchen and said "I believe you don't have anything to do with this; you were just in the wrong place, at the wrong time. So, I won't tear any of your things up. I'm just looking for drugs or anything that was a part of the investigation." I signed a paper noting this. He also asked questions about the co-defendants. I told him that I didn't know anything about those people. But the cop was dirty; he wrote his own statement that basically framed me as a *rat*. After finding nothing, the cop left the kitchen, as if he was convinced that I had nothing to do with it. After using his phone, he called me back into the kitchen, asking me if I would set up the other guy with a drug deal to get him caught. I made it clear that I didn't want to take the offer. The officer quickly told me if I didn't take the offer, I would be locked up within a week for conspiracy. I thought he was just kidding and trying to scare me into doing the job. What he was asking was very dangerous and I was thinking about the safety of my children.

I went to my friends' hearing at court. Within minutes of arriving, a couple of guys in suits approached me, confirmed my name, then swiftly escorted me to a cell. I was let out on bond, but a lawyer came with an indictment; I had been locked up because I refused to take the officer's deal. This is when I began to realize that my brother's girlfriend was an informant. They claimed that they witnessed her buying drugs from me a few days prior to the court hearing. I told them that I didn't sell drugs, but they had enough evidence against me.

The appeal started, but within four days, I was convicted of the charges. I was sentenced to 10-years incarceration and 10-years supervised release. All appeals were denied. My lawyers were ineffective. I served my time in a federal prison over 500 miles away from my home. While in prison, I turned my life over to God and was released as a new woman. **The Dope Game** had me trapped in my mind. The hood would not leave me alone. Now, it is God who has me and He won't leave me alone. *I am free and I am blessed!*

How Her Story Relates to My Story:

_____

_____

_____

_____

_____

_____

_____

_____

_____

_____

_____

_____

_____

_____

How Her Story Relates to My Story:

_____

_____

_____

_____

_____

_____

_____

_____

_____

_____

_____

_____

Author Felicia Brown

Felicia Brown

Felicia Brown was born in Cincinnati, Ohio and is currently residing in Waldorf, Maryland. She is a God-fearing woman, a mother of three, and a grandmother of two beautiful young ladies. Felicia Brown is also an entrepreneur. She has honorably served in the United States Navy for 20 years. Ms. Brown is the owner of Simply Yours by LISA. She is constantly pushing to learn more and more. She earned her diploma in Culinary Arts from the Arts Institute of Washington in 2014, a Master's in Public Administration (MPA) with a concentration in Public Policy and Management from Bowie State University in 2012, a Bachelor of Science and Certificate in Human Resource Management from the University of Maryland University College in 2010, and an Associate of Arts in Business and Management from the University of Maryland University College in 2007.

Ms. Brown's passion is helping the homeless and victims of abuse. She is the co-founder of iEndAbuse Foundation, a motivational speaker, and an Amazon best-selling author of a collaboration book named; *Born-overcomer: A Guide to Overcoming,* which is her author debut. Her family and a close circle of friends are extremely important! She loves to socialize whether that is at a cookout, playing spades, or just being around her friends and family! She has a zeal for swimming and likes to turn lemons into lemonade. She can find the positive in any situation. If she is not picking up a book to read, she will be mentoring young adults and crafting. She teaches several crafting activities online. She is a member of the Golden Key International Honour Society and the Illustrious Delta Sigma Theta Sorority, Incorporated.

Contact information: Website: simplyyoursbylisa.com
Email: Author.FeliciaBrown@gmail.com
Facebook: www.facebook.com/AuthorFeliciaBrown
Instagram: Author_Felicia_Brown

Built to Last

Joining the military at the ripe age of 18, I had no idea what was in store for me. I was told that I would be working on cars. Lo and behold, I was working on some of the largest diesel engines I had ever seen! When I left home to join the Navy, I didn't tell anyone that I was leaving. I was tired of following in my brother's footsteps. Throughout my entire schooling, I was told, "Your brother did this; your brother did that." I had earned a full ride to the Ohio State for Latin. However, when my best-friend said, "Hey, join the Navy with me." I was thinking, "Why not? I'm not going to college." I knew the only way for me to do this was to go behind my parents' back. So off to the Navy I went. We went on the "buddy" system; we were supposed to have been stationed together. Well, my friend went straight to the fleet in Pensacola, Florida and I went to Great Lakes for Engineman "A" School.

While I was there, I was one of only three females in the class. The school was a 14-week course that taught how to operate and repair diesel engines, distillate units, valves, pumps, heat exchangers, low-pressure air compressors, steam turbines, and hydraulic and pneumatic control devices. While I was going through training, I was hospitalized with the mumps, so this took me out of school for a while. Once I was able to return to class, I was placed with another group. In this group, I was the *only* female. Yet, I was #2 of the graduating class. I got my choice of orders. I picked London because that is what I was told. I wasn't told New London, Connecticut! They gave all the overseas billets to the males. If I only knew better.

I grew up in the hood, where it was up to you to survive. So, survival of the fittest has always been my way of life. When I first joined the military, I was still rough around the edges as far as what was coming out of my mouth. When I got to my first command in New London, Connecticut, I was told by my supervisor that I wouldn't make it through my first year in the Navy. He was sure that I would be kicked out of the Navy. Well, I've always been the one to prove people wrong. When you first enter the Navy, you must do 90 days of temporary duty, whether on a ship or onshore, it's called mess cranking. Mess cranking is when you work in the mess hall (cafeteria) bussing tables, washing dishes, doing all the messy work. On shore duty, you work at a building doing dirty work such as scrubbing baseboards or cleaning toilets. Well, I was stationed on shore duty. During my shore duty, a fellow sailor's cat died, and they gave her bereavement leave; I was blown away! A few weeks later, my Uncle transitioned, and they wouldn't allow me to go home for his funeral because he wasn't an *immediate* family member. I was torn up and I expressed my feelings. "How can you give someone leave for a cat and I can't take leave for my family member?" Their response was, "Well, a cat is an extension of a child." I went off with my mouth!

After my 90-day temporary duty, I was sent to my duty station. I was stationed on a tugboat as an engineer. However, when the station was short of people, I was assigned as the engineer on small MIC boats. On a tugboat, everyone must help on deck. At the time, I was 5'5", a size 3, weighing 146lbs, so I looked small. However, what people didn't know was that I lifted weights throughout high school. So, under my clothes, I was *cut up* like a diesel engine. I was told to go out on deck and help with the 4" line. We used this to dock and pull-out submarines. However, when the line is dropped in the water it feels like it's over 100 pounds. We had to bring the line on the deck by hand; afterwards, we used the winch to secure it. The first time I went out on deck to assist, the guys were like, "You won't be able to do this. Go back to your engineroom." Well, of course me being me, I had to show them- "Don't let my size fool you. I look small, but I'm a beast!" I jumped into the front and heaved that line up on the deck so fast. I shut their mouths; they would never underestimate me again!

While on this command, I was physically assaulted by my Chief Engineer. You know the saying- what happens here stays here. Well, the Navy has its own *good ole' boy* system. I really can't remember what started the argument, but I do know I didn't tolerate people talking down to me or disrespecting me. What I do remember is him picking me up and slamming my head into the wall. The only thing I could think of, at the time, was to spit in his face. So that's exactly what I did. He released his hold on me and I tried my best to kick him where it hurt. Then I ran. The other people who were on the boat at that time, ran after me to check on me. I went back to my barracks that day and cried myself to sleep. I got up the next day as if nothing had happened. I went to work; he went to work and never spoke to me again. However, what he did, was assign me duty on every holiday.

I got pregnant in my third year in the Navy at this command. While I was in my third trimester, the Chief Engineer told me to report to duty to shovel snow. I asked him, "Would you ask your wife to shovel snow while she is pregnant?" Then I hung up the phone. I was written up for not shoveling snow, but I didn't care.

Fast forward to my next duty station. I was stationed onboard the U.S.S. Yellowstone. I had to drop my baby off in Ohio with my mom. While I was in Ohio, there was a blizzard; so, I was late reporting to my command. I contacted my command and they understood. When I checked onboard, I discovered that I was the only female in my division. I worked in the Auxiliary Division better known as A-Gang. I was working on a heating unit and I asked for some assistance removing the coil. My supervisor told me, "I will not send anybody to assist you. You better start lifting some weights or something. We will not be helping you. I went back; I struggled to remove that hot, 80-pound coil. It dropped on my arm and I still have a small scar on my left arm to remind me that I can do anything I put my mind to. Don't allow anyone to stop your growth!

Being stationed onboard a ship, we must go out to sea. It could be from days to several months. My mother, oldest sister, and my baby met me on the pier after being gone for six months. Once the ship docked, my family came onboard. I was so excited to see them, especially my baby! I left her when she was only three months old. I reached for my baby... she cried and didn't want me to touch or hold her. This tore my heart to pieces; I ran down to my berthing area and just cried. I finally came back to my family and we went to the hotel. Once we arrived at the hotel, my baby still didn't want anything to do with me. It took several days for my baby to feel comfortable enough to let me hold her. While my family was visiting, I found a place to rent which was less than ten minutes from the base. I had my baby back with me. I needed to bond with my child, and I had to find a babysitter. Being a single parent is hard. However, being a single parent stationed on a ship is so much harder, especially when we go out to sea. I began asking people on the ship about babysitters; a shipmate's husband volunteered to watch my child until I could find a babysitter. I finally found a suitable babysitter and she had been watching my child for several months when the unexpected happened. While out to sea, I was told to go to the command center for an important message. Do you know…she sent me a message stating she could no longer watch my child starting that day. She didn't give me a reason, or anything. She just stated that she could no longer watch my child. I almost lost my mind; I'm out to sea, what was I going to do? I had a million things running through my mind. My family is in Ohio and I'm out to sea! There were no cell phones back then. We were using a POTS line: plain old telephone system. Everyone did not have access to this line. Since it was an emergency, they allowed me to use it. I'm still thinking what was I supposed to do? I'm in Virginia with no one…I had been in the area less than a year; I knew no one. I remembered a shipmate that stayed behind. I called her and she went and got my baby for me. She kept my daughter until I returned home. Fortunately, my shipmate's husband started watching my child once again.

I am now pregnant with my second child. I found a suitable babysitter that watched both of my children while I was at work and out to sea. She lived two houses down from me, her prices were reasonable, and the arrangement was so convenient. I thought I had hit the jackpot. She was so great! Then her prices increased drastically. I couldn't afford to pay the babysitter, provide food, pay rent, pay the car note and insurance. I was paying her more than I paid for rent! Was I getting help from my children's fathers? NO, absolutely not! Well, I retract that; I got help from my second child's father. Still, there was not enough money to pay for all the expenses of the household. I would eat on the ship, so I didn't have to eat when I got home, and I could just feed my children. No one knew what I was going through.

I finally broke down and I called my mother. I asked her if I could send my children to her. I explained that I would move back on the ship and send her my entire check and just keep $50 for myself until my time was up. Then I would move back home. My mother asked me, "Is this what you really want to do?" I replied, "No, because if I come home, all I'm going to do is get myself into trouble. There's nothing there for me." My mother surprised me! She retired early and came to live with me to help take care of my kids so I could keep my career.

My next command was the U.S.S. Hayler, homeported at Naval Station, Norfolk, Virginia. Once again, I was the only female in my division. Instead of having me working on equipment, they kept trying to make me an admin to do all the records, such as the engineering logbooks and other mediocre tasks. I refused to do them; I went to school and had just as much knowledge as everyone else. This Caucasian male told me, "You're never going to make rank. Look at you, who do you think you are?" That got under my skin, so I learned everything there was to know about that ship. My Lieutenant recognized my abilities and knowledge and made me their supervisor. That ate them up, so they kept trying to sabotage everything to make me look bad. I had to have a *Come-to-Jesus* moment with myself. I realized that most of the women on the ship who were in the engineering department were experiencing similar issues. Our issues were babysitting, being assigned administrative work, and men trying to make us feel inferior to them.

I started meeting with other females so we could all be on the same accord and help each other. They taught me and I taught them. But the best part was my mother started watching everyone's children for them because she knew our struggle. They no longer had to worry about what they were going to do with their children when we went out to sea. We are all still great friends to this day. Actually, we are closer than that; we are family!

Did I mention, I now have three children. The saga continued we got a new Chief Engineer onboard, and he was a no-nonsense type of man. He had no heart! We had to work through Christmas Eve and Christmas to prepare for an upcoming inspection.

However, it didn't take us working around the clock to get prepared. My youngest child's grandmother passed away and I wanted…well, I needed to go to the funeral. Her funeral was in the Tidewater area; and therefore, did not require distant travel. Yet I was told that I could not go because she was not in my immediate family. She was my daughter's grandmother! Once again, I felt the same way I felt when this same excuse was given to me during my first command. How can this be? I was hurt! She and I were really close…she called me her daughter. I told the Chief Engineer exactly what was on my mind and then I told him that I was leaving the Navy! I walked off the ship and proceeded home. I told my mom I was done! I contacted my detailer and told him I was leaving and the reason why. So, I started processing out of the Navy. My Lieutenant called my detailer and told them they couldn't afford to lose me. However, I applied for a job in Maryland. I went to the interview and on-the-spot, I was offered a research and development position with Baltimore Aircoil Company. On my way back to Virginia, I received a call from my detailer. He asked me to please stay in; they would give me the time that I needed for bereavement and I could be transferred to a new command. Needless to say, I stayed, attended the funeral, and then transferred to Annapolis, Maryland.

Fast forward five years later, we are now stationed in San Diego, California. I had to leave my babies at 3:00 am on Easter morning. I didn't even get a chance to see them wake up! I left to meet my ship in Bahrain, a country in the Middle East! When my youngest daughter saw me coming off the ship after being gone for nine months, she peed all over herself because she was so excited to see me.

Yes! I made it to my last duty station at Washington Navy Yard, DC. At last, I'm able to spend some quality time with my three children. My youngest daughter had just started elementary school, my son and oldest daughter were off to middle school. My mother stayed with me this entire journey. Throughout my twelve years as an Engineman, I was able to go from a ranking of E1 to E6 and retire as Personnel Specialist First Class Petty Officer (Surface Warfare/ Aviation Warfare). This command gave me a whole new view on harassment.

My sacrifice for this country came at a great cost; it resulted in my strained relationship with my oldest daughter. Looking back, I wondered would I have done anything different. I would say, no, because God has ordered my steps and I was built for a time such as this! No words can describe the love that I have for my children! I sacrificed so that they never have too.

How Her Story Relates to My Story:

_____

_____

_____

_____

_____

_____

_____

_____

_____

_____

_____

_____

_____

Gerly Sapphire Harris

Gerly Sapphire Harris

Gerly Sapphire Harris was born and raised in Brooklyn, New York and currently resides in the nation's capital. Mrs. Harris is married and has one awesome son, and currently works at the United States Department of Health and Human Services, under the Health Resources and Services Administration (HRSA), although this job does not adequately describe all of who she is. Mrs. Harris is an advocate of woman's health and she is a proponent of the inclusion of all populations, especially individuals from Culture of People with Disabilities. The disability culture is a growing and dynamic community that is often overlooked as it relates to the promotion of good health, education, and women's empowerment.

As a person with a physical disability, Mrs. Harris realizes that she can positively impact society by conducting workshops, participating in conferences, and joining various women organizations to help break through barriers and demolish stereotypes. Mrs. Harris has come to understand that her success as a woman with a disability could help inspire people from all walks of life. Mrs. Harris' desire to help others and make a difference in the world is far more than a whim; it is a passion. Mrs. Harris is currently pursuing my Doctorate in Psychology, and she is a lifetime member of Psi Chi International Honor Society in Psychology. Mrs. Harris has a Masters in Educational Psychology from Howard University, and a Bachelor's Degree in Professional Studies. She has done extensive research on the disability culture and tutored youths with disabilities.

Mrs. Harris has also conducted presentations at numerous conferences and forums pertaining to the disability culture throughout the Washington DC Metropolitan area and in New York. She is the former Washington, DC Chapter President for the National Association of Professional Women organization. She is currently the Executive Director for the National Congress of Black Women, Incorporated (NCBW) Maryland State Chapter College for Kids (CFK) and College for Teens Programs. These programs are used to introduce young people to traditional and non-traditional occupations. Mrs. Harris is the National Committee Chair for the NCBW Culture of People with

Disabilities Committee. She co-chaired the Training Committee for the First Baptist Church of Glenarden (FBCG) Special Needs Ministry and was the Editor-in-Chief for the Ministry's newsletter. She is committed to children because they are precious and represent the future.

Mrs. Harris currently sits on the Board and was the former President for the Kiwanis Club of Northwest Washington, DC, and currently the President Elect for the Kiwanis Club of Far East where the focus area of both Clubs is catered towards the empowerment of children with disabilities. Mrs. Harris is the former Editor-in-Chief for the Blacks in Government, Parklawn Chapter newsletter, and former Vice-President for the Eta Phi Beta Sorority Incorporated, Epsilon Epsilon Chapter. Mrs. Harris is currently the President for the HRSA Employee Resource Group, Council on Employees with Disabilities. Mrs. Harris is an active member of National Active and Retired Federal Employees Association (NARFE) and the chapter's National Legislation Chair, as well as an active member of the Metropolitan Women's Democratic Club. Mrs. Harris is an active member with the Daughters, an Auxiliary of Ancient Egyptian Arabic Order Nobles Mystic Shrine (AEONMS), Order of the Eastern Star, and writes for the Grand Lodge of the District of Columbia, Incorporated, in the Prince Hall Masonic Digest. She has a burning passion for the country of Haiti and Haitian people worldwide. She has traveled to Haiti as a part of a political envoy, and she tirelessly works with different organizations to help improve the quality of life for the great citizens of Haiti. She has also traveled to South African in a missionary capacity and to Europe for educational and missionary purposes.

Mrs. Harris received awards for her hard work and dedication from Blacks in Government, Parklawn Chapter, National Congress of Black Women, National Association of Professional Women, Health Resources and Services Administration Employee Resource Group, and Men Aiming Higher, Incorporated, just to name a few. Mrs. Harris continues to be a positive Social Change Agent for the Culture of People with Disabilities.

Understanding Difference

I am different from you – yes I am
Stop telling me that, we're the same.
Someday you'll see and learn
That I am different from you and we're not the same.
One day I hope you'll understand
How difficult it really was for me to stand.
I am different from you,
Please take heed and understand that at least,
And accept my differences
And be cognizant of my physical dissimilarities.
Don't be like those who try to convince others
To modify their life styles.
Accept me for who I am
A person who is different,
Different and not ashamed.
I am different from you, unique in every way,
So stop telling me that, we're the same every day.
Take the time to understand my difference,
But not from a distance.
And learn to appreciate that everyone
In essence, has some type of uniqueness.
Being physically different doesn't mean
That we don't share the same interests and needs.
But keep in mind of struggles and the pain
That we share from within, are the same indeed.
All I am asking is for you to understand,
For equal respect of our differences at hand.
For equal opportunity and equal accessibility
For an understanding of the uniqueness
Of the culture of physical disability.

Understanding Difference

W hen I look back on how my life started and where I am now, gratitude fills my heart. I am a first-generation American and the youngest of seven children. I was born and raised in Brooklyn New York. My parents immigrated to the United States from the Caribbean in search of a better life. Once my parents settled in Brooklyn, they began working towards establishing a foundation for a family legacy. My parents purchased, owned, and managed an apartment building which taught us the importance of ownership, self-sufficiency, and service.

I was born with one leg shorter than the other, and other physical abnormalities, which included Spinal Bifida and Scoliosis. I was three days old when I had my first surgery, undertaken to correct the unusual way my leg had developed. My parents spent an enormous amount of time in hospitals, speaking and consulting with medical specialists. Growing up, I had several surgeries, although none had the desired outcome of correcting the abnormalities of my spine or the length of my leg. Spending time in hospitals before speaking my first words had a massive residual impact on my life. It was impossible to attend school in a traditional manner when much of my energy was consumed with medical treatments. The physical challenges faced as an infant and during my early years lead many of the medical professionals working with me, to believe that I would never walk. They felt so strongly that they encouraged my parents to begin planning for my life accordingly. While my parents were grateful for the efforts of the doctors who worked on my behalf, they were unwilling to accept their diagnosis. As a result, the battle for mobility and a more conventional life continued. During my last surgery about the age of seven, it was nearly fatal; I flat-lined during the procedure. It felt as if, a part of me started transitioning to the next level of spiritual existence, while a part of me remained rooted in this dimension. As I got older and developed a greater understanding of God's Word, I believe that it was the Grace of God that brought me back to life. Once again, the doctors told my parents, that I would never walk, but their faith led them to believe that God had a purpose and a special plan for my life. Decades later, I am still walking, and walking with all my appendages.

At an age when most children were preparing for pre-kindergarten, I was engaged in one of my earliest battles of doing what experts said I could not do. Education in the traditional sense was not possible for me. In retrospect, this was probably a good thing because I also had a speech impediment. I was home-schooled for most of my formative years and learned to walk and talk in an environment filled with faith and love. My childhood was filled with challenges, such as learning to walk and speak without stuttering, while kids my age were playing. One of the most important lessons I learned was, being different was okay. Just because people may look, walk, talk, or think differently than the majority of people, there was nothing wrong with that. While this was the way I tried to live my life, people have not always extended the same in return. When I was walking, some people would stare or make inappropriate comments towards me; as a child, I did not fully understand why. I have always attempted to live the lessons taught to me by my parents, which was to love everyone and give people the benefit of doubt. I was raised to love, respect, and accept me for who I am, and not accept the negative opinions of others. The trajectory of my life would have been so much different if my parents and my environment would have let me settle for less than the best.

What I began to recognize as a child was, that I was not like "everyone" else. My family loved and sheltered me, making sure that I was not being treated differently because of my physical differences. The word disability was seldom mentioned in my household, my parents encouraged me to be fearless and experiment with the things I wanted to do, such as tap dance, ballet, and skating. They taught me that the only person that could stop me, was me. As a result, I believed that I could conquer anything.

I remember my first day attending Catholic school. I had to wear orthopedic combat boots, and a few kids made fun of my shoes. When I got home, I told my parents, that week my father found an orthopedic shoe store in Manhattan and brought a customized orthopedic boot that I was so proud to wear. My siblings would often beat up kids who made fun of me, which prevented others from making the same mistake. I knew that my family would not always be there to protect me, so I searched to connect with people who, through their own personal experiences, understood some of the challenges that I faced daily, as a person with a physical disability. This was not an easy undertaking. For many years, I was unable to find a role model, a mentor, or anyone in leadership that had a disability. Napoleon Hill, the famous author of 'Think and Grow Rich' said, 'In every adversity lies the seed of an equal or greater opportunity,' which was definitely true in my case. The exclusion I felt from the lack of disabled role models inspired me to make a positive difference within my community. I grew up not learning much about the type of disability that I was born with, but deep in my heart, I was yearning to learn. I started college and focused on leadership, so I would be well equipped to assist individuals with a disability.

Once I graduated and moved on, I experienced the greater success Napoleon Hill spoke of during my time as a graduate student at Howard University. It is there that the arc of my life would change, as I crossed paths with someone who would help change my destiny. During the first semester of my graduate program, I found what I had been searching for most of my life, a mentor. Dr. Sylvia Walker was a professor and the director of the Howard University Research and Training Center, Socio Economic for People with Disabilities. Dr. Walker was legally blind from childhood, but she could see me, and the world much better than any person with 20/20 vision that I had ever met. She helped me on a professional and a personal level. My family instilled in me, the belief that I could do and accomplish anything; however, it was Dr. Walker that placed wings on that belief, and I have been soaring ever since. Dr. Walker was so congruent in what she believed, what she said, and what she taught me; I believed I could bend reality. I learned a lot during my years at Howard University under her guidance, about disability, politics, and being an advocate, which positioned me to be the influential voice for people with disabilities. Having her as my mentor provided me with a wider knowledge of the culture of people with disabilities. My family did not raise me as a person with a disability, nor did my environment consist of people with disabilities. I always had the desire to know more about the dynamic culture of people with a disability, because I was a part of the culture and was not ashamed. Dr. Walker was so impactful, that I not only wanted to be like her, but I wanted to become the powerful instrumental woman that I was created to be. Our relationship reminds me of Laubach's theory, "each one, teach one." My mentor and I attended various conferences and workshops dealing with people with disabilities, and on several occasions, she was the keynote speaker. We even met the President of the United State, who was Bill Clinton at that time, during a disability program held at the White House. As a result, I began to learn more and explore more about the culture of people with disabilities. As a graduate student at Howard University under Dr. Walker's leadership, I conducted extensive research on the culture of people with disabilities, tutored youths with disabilities, and presented at several conferences and forums pertaining to the disability culture. These forums were held throughout the Metropolitan Area of Washington, DC, New York, and throughout the east coast.

I never saw myself as a game-changer or as someone who would ever be recognized for their efforts. My only desire has been to make a positive difference in the world, by helping to make life a little better for those individuals with a disability. Game changers are people who see a need and do something positive to revolutionize it in such a way that others would want to be a part. They decide to set aside feelings of insecurity and fear, to trust in doing the impossible. My desire to help others is more than a whim; it is a passion. The culture of people with disabilities is a growing and dynamic community that is often overlooked at programs that promote health, education, and women empowerment. This passion has challenged me to help make change for people with disabilities a reality; I speak for some women who may not be in a position to speak for themselves. As the former President of the National Association of Professional Women (NAPW) Washington, DC Chapter, I worked to create an atmosphere for women that was conducive to personal growth and development. As a Chapter, our organization provided educational workshops for women who resided in shelters or would be considered a part of a low-income family. Under my leadership, the NAPW Washington, DC Chapter participated in fundraisers, quarterly Outreach endeavors, worked to create environments that fostered networking, provided makeovers to low-income families, provided clothing to disabled families, and partnered with other community-based organizations to bring about positive change within the community. The membership base for NAPW Washington, DC Chapter tripled in size under my presidency. Working towards empowerment, and building a solid foundation that promoted disability awareness, were aspirational goals of mine. I joined other prominent organizations such as the National Congress of Black Women Incorporated, and the Kiwanis International Club, to bring about disability awareness.

I am very passionate about serving communities outside of the United States as well, one country in particular, is Haiti. I am constantly seeking and working with different organizations to help improve the quality of life for the citizens of Haiti. I have traveled to Haiti as a part of the political envoy with the former Mayor of District Heights, Maryland. I participated in fund-raising efforts, following the earthquake in Haiti that took place in 2010. Haiti is a land that is rich in human ability and talent, although the individuals tapping into these resources have not always had the best interest of the citizens in mind. My goal has been to provide resources and help bring about disability awareness. My family encouraged me to believe that I could do anything and should not allow my disability to hinder my progress or efforts in any way. My family also believed that having a good education would help open doors for me, that the lack of understanding as it relates to people with a disability might attempt to close. Since then, I have always believed that education was one way that I could influence change. It is my desire to educate, empower, encourage, and heighten awareness of the culture of people with disabilities, which will foster an understanding of differences.

I was fortunate to have crossed paths with my first mentor, Dr. Walker, whose impact is still being felt in my life up until this very day. While mentors or role models were not plentiful, another person that I learned about and admired was Sojourner Truth. When we look at the time period in which Sojourner Truth lived, the obstacles she faced, the cruelty she overcame, the heartache of slavery that she felt, and then look at her accomplishments, we know that it was God who inspired her to pursue liberation for herself, her family, for women, and for all African Americans. Sojourner Truth was a woman of perseverance and faith. Sojourner Truth battled the court system for her son and won. Sojourner Truth battled the definition of womanhood and won. Sojourner Truth may not have been the one society would have chosen to lead, but she is the one that God chose. Bringing this to the present, you may have had challenges in your life that you believed disqualified you, but not so. You may have thought your mistakes may have disqualified you, but not so. God placed a treasure in your heart, and He has given you all the gifts you need to manifest it. Because Sojourner Truth stood up and said '*Ain't I a Woman*?' I can use my God-given gifts and talents to inspire individuals with a disability and make a positive difference in the world. As a person with a disability, through my personal experiences and desire to educate others, I hope to help revolutionize the perception and the image of the culture of people with disabilities, while simultaneously providing a model worthy of emulation. Because Sojourner Truth lived her life, I can be all that God called and predestined me to be. Long live the Spirit of Sojourner Truth and all those who paved the way!

How Her Story Relates to My Story:

_____

_____

_____

_____

_____

_____

_____

_____

_____

_____

_____

_____

How Her Story Relates to My Story:

_____

_____

_____

_____

_____

_____

_____

_____

_____

_____

_____

_____

_____

_____

Author Dr. Karen Reddick-Bolden

Dr. Karen Reddick-Bolden

Dr. Karen Reddick-Bolden was born in Thomasville, Georgia, grew up in Greenville, Florida and have been residing in Memphis, Tennessee since 2017. Karen is engaged to Mr. Larry McDaniel. She has two daughters, Angilquente, the youngest, and Ebony the oldest who is married to Joe Wilbert. They have four children Dillion, Dejah, De'Shaun, and Destinee.

Karen served 32 years in the United States Army as a Chaplain Assistant. While serving in the military Karen earned her Doctorate Degree in Ministry and a Master's Degree in Religion. She also received numerous awards and decorations. Karen always connected with a local ministry at each duty station using her gifts in the areas of Leadership and Teaching, Preaching, Praise and Worship, and Youth Ministry. Karen also coins herself as a Health and Fitness guru. She is a Personal Trainer and she has an online business that specializes in health and fitness products and overall wellness.

After retiring from the military in 2016 Karen became a JROTC Senior Army Instructor. When asked during her interview why she wanted to be a JROTC Instructor, Karen said that growing up she always had a passion to teach. She went on to say that she served as a Training Manager while in the military at several duty stations and ultimately served at the United States Army Training and Doctrine Command – Fort Eustis, Virginia. Karen feels that becoming a JROTC Senior Army Instructor and mentoring and coaching High School students was a natural progression to what she did in the military as a Senior NCO.

Karen has a heart for God and the people of God. Her deepest desire is to use her God given talents, time, and treasures to impact those that God place in her path and for them to see and know the God that lives within her.

Surviving the Domino Effect of Life's Trials and Tribulations

And they overcame him by the blood of the Lamb, and by the word of their testimony... Revelation 12:11a [KJV]

I used to think that I did not have a testimony, but I eventually came to believe that my story, both the good and the challenging, *is* my testimony. Someone once told me that whatever your story is, "own it" because someone out there needs to hear it and so, this is my story – this is my testimony.

My parents were very strict, and they raised my siblings and me in a Christian home. I was the youngest of ten siblings and I have a twin sister, Kathi. I was rebellious growing up because of the strict environment. But, later in life, I appreciated my upbringing. Although I was rebellious, I did what I was supposed to in school; made good grades and graduated.

I grew up in a small town called Greenville, Florida. The population has always been under 1000. A very small town without much to do. My parents did not allow us to date, but I did without their knowledge until at the age of 14, I became pregnant and gave birth to my daughter, Ebony. When I realized I was pregnant, I was very much afraid of how my parents might respond. So, I hid my pregnancy from them until I could no longer keep it a secret. My parents were hurt, and I hated that I had caused that pain. Once they got over the shock of their "baby girl" being pregnant, they supported me wholeheartedly. Some of the people in my hometown had negative things to say about me. Very few had encouraging or positive words. However, I do remember the things my brother's wife, Henrietta said to me. Because what she said to me set me on a course that day that changed my life. It also cultivated within me an attitude that I had something to prove to everyone who had negative words and I had to make my parents proud of me. Henrietta said, "Hold your head up. You are not the first teenager to get pregnant. Do not allow this to define the rest of your life. You can still do positive things in your life." I don't think Henrietta knew the magnitude of what she spoke into my life that day and maybe she did, but she was so right. She spoke it and God brought it into existence. *As it is written, I have made thee a father of many nations, before him whom he believed, even God, who quickeneth the dead, and calleth those things which be not as though they were.* Romans 4:17 [KJV]

I was a freshman during my pregnancy, and I attended high school until I went into early labor. Ebony was a happy child, and I kept her close. Her biological father was not a constant in her life. I was out of school for six to eight weeks recovering. Little did I know God was working things out for my good so that I would graduate on time. You see, my county had a program called Homebound. "Homebound instruction – not to be confused with homeschooling – is a temporary solution for students who cannot attend class for a variety of reasons. The purpose is to give students the opportunity to stay current with their studies with educator-approved learning materials, as well as in-person tutoring or instruction." At that time in 1980, giving birth was one of those reasons a student could take advantage of Homebound Instruction. However, the school board later decided that giving birth would no longer be accepted for Homebound Instruction. I was the last teenage mother to take advantage of Homebound Instruction. God worked it out for my good! Now, I had to think about my daughter and her provisions. That was the main reason I decided not to go to college immediately after high school but join the military instead. That and the fact that I did not want my parents having the responsibility of taking care of me and my daughter. The military was exactly where God destined me to be. *"For I know the plans I have for you," declares the LORD, "plans to prosper you and not to harm you, plans to give you hope and a future." Jeremiah 29:11 [KJV]*

In 1984 I joined the military as a Chaplain Assistant. My parents adopted my daughter so that I could join the Army. The understanding was that I was coming back home to get her after my training. My first duty station was in Germany. Being there acclimated me to the Army. Although there were some challenges, there were also many accomplishments. It was also where I grew closer to God. During my second duty station, at Fort Rucker, Alabama, I went back home and relocated my daughter to be with me. Being a single parent was not easy, but the Lord always provided what we needed. The Lord connected me to a great church family. My daughter grew and flourished!

My way of proving to all the naysayers in my hometown that I would not end up as they predicted was to submit a Hometown News Release every single time I accomplished something in the Army. Promotions, awards, special training, it was all in my Hometown newspaper! You can say that those news releases tracked my career from start to finish! *"I can do all things through Christ which strengtheneth me." Philippians 4:13 [KJV]*

While at Fort Rucker, Alabama, I met and married my husband in 1988. He raised my daughter, Ebony as his own. We left Fort Rucker, Alabama and went back to Germany. We connected with another great church family and our faith began to grow. There we had another daughter, who we call Angil. She was for sure a "daddy's girl". A delightful and happy child. Although she and Ebony would get into sibling arguments often, by all accounts we had the perfect family. We did not know that there would be challenges on the horizon that would seem impossible to maneuver. They would come like a domino effect. *"Now we can see that You know all things and that You do not even need to have anyone ask You questions. This makes us believe that You came from God." John 16: 30 [NIV]*

So, domino number one, in 1990 before leaving Germany I was scheduled to deploy until I had an abnormal pap smear and the doctor found precancerous cells on my uterus and I had to have emergency surgery. As a result, I could no longer deploy. This did not go over well with my leadership. People appeared to be genuinely concerned for me, yet when I would hear gossip about comments that were being made, I really did not know how genuinely concerned people were.

We left Germany and went to Fort Riley, Kansas. As I signed into my unit, one of the Caucasian NCOs noticed my rank of Staff Sergeant and how young I looked. He asked me in a very serious voice, "Whose butt did you kiss", to which I replied very sternly, "God's!" After that interaction, I did not have to worry about that NCO. Although there were definitely others like him, which was just another domino I had to deal with. Later, my marriage came under attack. We were no longer that "perfect" family. Then I had to leave my family and go to Korea. I did not know why God was allowing this to happen when we were already in a bad place. All I could see was that another domino had fallen.

I made it to Korea and the job ahead of me was no easy task. This was the next domino. The previous Senior NCO who I replaced was going through a Court Martial for gross dereliction of duty. He was the Fund Manager responsible for a million-dollar fund. By the time I arrived the fund was close to being bankrupt. The Fund Clerk was also being Court Martial for stealing funds. My job was to clean it up and serve as an expert witness in the case of the Fund Clerk. It took my first year there to clean it up and my second year to maintain it. Through that ordeal, I developed a heart condition and several other health concerns. My family did join me that second year but the problems in my marriage were still there. Not only that, Ebony was now a teenager and had become very rebellious. She was often cited for truancy; eventually, my Command ordered me to send her back to the United States. *"For I will restore health unto thee, and I will heal thee of thy wounds, saith the Lord; because they called thee an Outcast, saying, This is Zion, whom no man seeketh after." Jeremiah 30:17 [KJV]*

I did not know where God was in all of this. I felt as though He had abandoned me. I tried to find comfort in Hebrews 13:5 where the Apostle Paul said that He (God) will never leave you or forsake you. But then we were called to Angil's school. We were informed by her teacher that Angil assaulted her. I asked the teacher when this occurred, she said in November, but we were now in January. I said, "No way am I punishing my daughter, a third-grader, for something you say she did three months ago. We should have been informed." The teacher said Angil needed to be prescribed Ritalin (methylphenidate). "Ritalin is a central nervous system stimulant prescribed for treating narcolepsy (uncontrollable sleepiness), and attention-deficit hyperactivity disorder (ADHD)." The teacher also said if we did not speak with the school counselor about the medication and the situation, Angil might be suspended. The teacher said she had reported the incident to the Principal. Still, no one had informed us. We met with the school counselor and declined to move forward with Ritalin. We later found out that several students in my daughter's class had been prescribed Ritalin. These were just more falling dominos, but this one ended in Victory. *Hallelujah! "But thanks be to God, which giveth us the victory through our Lord Jesus Christ." 1 Corinthians 15:57[KJV]*

Fort Carson, Colorado is where one of the major storms in my life would occur. In 1999, I started having headaches every day for a month. I finally decided to go to the doctor, but by then my eyesight began to decrease until I went blind! I didn't know what was going on. That was the beginning of a season of seeing one specialist after another: seeking to find a diagnosis. Finally, the doctors explained that I had inflammation on my left optic nerve, and it was causing me to go blind. When the same thing started attacking my right eye my doctors informed me that in order to save my sight in my right eye, they had to do surgery. The same surgery they do to remove a brain aneurism. I had aggressive bilateral optic neuritis: an auto-immune disease. Surrounded by my family, my brother, Wendell, and his family, and lots of sisters in Christ praying, I made it through the surgery. The doctors did not get the results they were hoping for, but they could tell that it was not a tumor or cancer. Praise God! Although it was not a tumor or cancer, I had to be treated with the medicine they give to cancer patients plus two forms of steroids which brought on other issues. It was difficult to stay positive. It was hard to stay focused.

During treatment, my husband deployed, Ebony graduated, and joined the Air Force and Angil and I moved to Fort Sill, Oklahoma. Although I could not make sense of what was occurring, I began to see God's hand in my situation. You see, one of my brothers lived in Colorado and one of my sisters, Edwina lived in Oklahoma. God was connecting me with family. He also connected me with a ministry that was instrumental in my time of rest, because only God knew what was ahead. My time at Fort Sill, Oklahoma was very short; it was my place of refuge. As we go through the battle it is necessary to take a knee and just allow God to fill us with His peace and restoration. God also blessed me to be selected for Sergeant Major and selected to attend the United States Army Sergeants Major Academy, at Fort Bliss, Texas. *"Come unto me, all ye that labour and are heavily laden, and I will give you rest." Matthew 11: 28 [KJV]*

After completing the Sergeants Major Academy, I was selected to deploy but because of the aggressive bilateral optic neuritis, I could not deploy. Some of my peers began to say negative things about me not deploying; only a few of my closest friends knew what I was going through. It caused me to feel a certain way, but I just had to ignore the noise. The Lord allowed me to complete the Sergeants Major Academy and earn my Doctorate degree in Ministry. My husband and I decided that since he had retired and since Angil was a junior in high school, they would remain at Fort Bliss, Texas while I moved to San Antonio, Texas. They would join me once Angil graduated. Well, it did not occur quite that way, and little did I know, I was about to experience another falling domino.

I moved to San Antonio, Texas as my husband and I planned. However, shortly after my move, the enemy launched an all-out attack on my marriage and my family that did not end well. Unfortunately, after 21 years of marriage, my husband and I divorced. The circumstances surrounding my divorce were something you would only see in a Netflix Drama Series! It was a very difficult time for Angil and me. It was only by the grace of God that we got through it all: but not without many battle wounds, scars, and lifelong effects. I fell into a state of depression; yet it was my daughter, Angil who was affected the most. She ended up coming to live with me. I can tell you that it was only the Lord that enabled me to heal and eventually minister to other women.

My eyesight was partially restored in one of my eyes. However, in 2010 while stationed with my daughter, Angil in Korea for another tour, I once again went totally blind. This time it occurred in both eyes at the same time. Initially, I was angry and afraid. Then the Lord had to remind me concerning His word. *"For God hath not given us the spirit of fear; but of power, and of love, and of a sound mind."* 2 *Timothy 1:7 [KJV]*

God reminded me of the individuals he had placed in my life: my pastors, one of my peers, and my daughter. I was eventually sent back to the United States before my tour officially ended to be treated at Walter Reed Hospital and Bethesda Naval Hospital. I was assigned to a Warrior Transitional Unit. By this time, I had a lot of uncertainty about my career. I was a Sergeant Major with approximately 27 years in the Army and I wasn't ready to retire. My oldest sister, Mary, lived in Washington DC at that time which was another one of God's blessings. She, her friends, and her church family took care of me while I was there. Then God moved me to my final assignment in the Army, The United States Army Training and Doctrine Command, Fort Belvoir, Virginia. He connected me to a great ministry and a very loving church family who again, took care of me.

Despite all the uncertainties and challenges that I faced in my life journey, I can look back and see the hand of God leading and guiding me. I can see the blessings of God in my life. Despite being blind, God allowed me to touch the lives of others through ministry and through my testimony. He allowed me to serve 32 years and to start a second career as a JROTC Instructor in Memphis, Tennessee. Since teaching, God has allowed me to be selected as Senior Army Instructor of the Year. The greatest blessing from God is my fiancée, Larry McDaniel: a true man of God that loves and supports me. Thank you, Lord!

If you are going through trials and tribulations, if your dominos are falling, one after another, trust God to get you through. Use your trials and tribulations as a launching pad to rappel you into your next phase: into your destiny!

How Her Story Relates to My Story:

_____

_____

_____

_____

_____

_____

_____

_____

_____

_____

_____

_____

Author Katrina L. Strand

Katrina L. Strand

Katrina L. Strand is originally from Cocoa, Florida and currently resides in White Plains. She graduated from Cocoa High School in 1994 and went on active-duty in the Army in 1995. She enjoys spending time with her family and making memories while on vacation. Katrina has been married to J.E. Strand for more than thirteen years. Together they have a blended family that consists of nine children; Darrion, Monte, Marquez, Alexis, Ashanti, Jeffrey, Jekasia, Ray, and James III (Trey). Katrina is also blessed to have eight grandchildren.

Providing service to others is both her passion and her purpose. She is an Army Veteran who continues to serve her community even after her commitment to our nation. She enjoys not only giving financially through her charitable donations but giving of her time to those who need and desire help. She belongs to several charitable groups, including masonic organizations and a military sorority, all that promote charitable giving and community service as part of their mission statements. Katrina is also the founder of a non-profit organization, S.O.S. (Shifting of Situations) for Teen Moms Inc.

Katrina holds a B.S. in Psychology and a B.S. in Criminal Justice from Drury University, both graduating Magna Cum Laude. While working for the Department of Defense, Katrina obtained her Defense Acquisition Workforce Improvement Act (DAWIA) Level III Certification in Industrial Contract Property Management, Level I Life Cycle Logistics and Program Management from the Defense Acquisition University (DAU). Katrina is a member of the Defense Acquisition Corps; National Council of Negro Women (NCNW) Incorporated; Order of the Eastern Star (OES) PHA, Maryland and Jurisdiction Marjorie T. Lancaster Chapter #84, A.E.A.O.N.M.S, MISR Court #193 and Kappa Epsilon Psi Military Sorority Incorporated.

As a debut author, Katrina was somewhat nervous to share her story. After considerable prayer and authority from God to move forward; she understood that her story would be of encouragement and strength for someone dealing with domestic violence while suffering in silence. She acknowledged that God brought her through and although she may have been broken for a period of her life, God blessed her mess.

Katrina says that- "The thing I want others to get out of this chapter is that domestic violence is not age restrictive or restrictive to only marriages; it can be seen in various forms. Fortunately, there are a multitude of organizations available that you can seek help from. You do not have to suffer in silence."

Instagram: https://www.instagram.com/spcboo/?hl=en
Twitter: https://twitter.com/spcboo
Facebook: https://www.facebook.com/katrina.strand.3

Broken to Blessed

As my blood rushed down to my brain, and yes, I said down not up; I could remember hearing my cousin pleading for my safety. As my husband dangled me by my ankles over the second story of the barracks balcony, in my mind I kept saying "he'll never do anything to really hurt me." In case you're wondering what the barracks are, it's the place where the single soldiers lived on the military base. Your next question should be, "Why was my husband living in the single soldiers' quarters on the base?" Simply put, we had been involved in so many physical disputes that we had a no-contact order, and he was required to move out of our home and stay in the single soldiers' quarters. In a way, I felt that this current issue was my fault. If I had not "popped up" on him, I would not have caught him entertaining another young lady. When I realized his infidelity, I got loud and embarrassed him, thus causing him to take drastic measures! At least that's what I told myself.

This type of behavior became second nature to me; it was more like a common occurrence. We were both Command-directed to Anger Management treatment for one year to try to help us better understand our triggers and how to prevent those occurrences. At the time, I didn't understand that the name for what I was experiencing was called Domestic Violence. The term was first shared when my counselor explained the cycle. I still wasn't willing to admit that I was involved in a domestic violence situation. I felt that I was smart enough to recognize the difference between minor spousal fights and domestic violence and would have the foresight to leave when things became too bad. However, the unfortunate truth was that I had been involved for so many years that I had become conditioned and complacent.

I had been making excuses for all the unacceptable behaviors over the years. I kept telling myself that I was staying for my children. I convinced myself that their relationship with their father was more important than my sanity. I thought it was my responsibility as a mother to make the sacrifice for my children. In actuality, I was exposing them to abuse. Their happiness and childhood were being tarnished by witnessing my husband and me in frequent arguments about adultery, engaging in physical altercations, throwing and breaking objects, and shouting profanity at each other. These repeated inappropriate behaviors created a cycle of emotional abuse for my children. I had to ask myself, "How are you really helping them?" I found myself at a crossroads. Finally, I divorced my husband.

To everyone's dismay, after ninety short days of being divorced, I remarried my ex-husband! He kept telling me that he missed his family and wanted his family back and that he would do right. With all the things said, he never said that he would do better by me or that he would do better as a husband. Even without the full promise of rededication, I decided to give him another chance. Of course, this was very short-lived. I became pregnant with my third child and remembered getting a call from a long-time friend who announced they had traveled from overseas for his wife to deliver their first child at a local hospital. I went to visit the couple and their newborn; apparently, I stayed longer than my husband had expected me to stay. Upon my arrival back home, I was chased into my bathroom under a physical attack, and I was six months pregnant! My co-worker's husband had to rush to the home to calm my husband down because he had busted the doors down to the bedroom and bathroom, trying to physically attack me. Again, as horrifying as the abuse was and as innocent as my actions had been, I blamed myself. I thought that maybe I shouldn't have been out so long. I now realize that self-guilt is part of the domestic abuse cycle.

By the time that I left Texas to head overseas, my husband had been involved in so many different affairs with so many different women. He had two confirmed children and possibly a third child outside of our marriage. I was ready to leave, not only the state but the country because of the huge embarrassment. We separated yet again.

My husband became engaged to another young lady, while we were still married. I relocated to Europe on military assignment to start a new life. The ironic thing about this move was that I was also moving to Europe where the young man who was considered "the love of my life" resided. This made my husband feel insecure. Once he caught wind of my move, he had his orders changed from his original assignment. I guess I thought that this would be our opportunity to make things better; so once again, we reconciled. And once again, I found myself living in hell on earth. Here I was again, thinking I was too smart for my own good! I won't justify my actions, but after a few years of constant humiliation, I decided to take my life back.

My husband had such an enormous amount of stinking thinking about the "love of my life", not because I gave him a reason to, but because he was doing so much flawed and immoral stuff himself. My husband was back to his old ways of sleeping around and this time, he was taking it to a new level. He became sexually involved with a young lady that was frequently riding to work with me, and he was videotaping their escapade! They always say that you won't accuse someone of something that you're not doing or haven't done and that's exactly what he was doing! After a while of being accused, I self-indulged, I began to have an affair. I had made up my mind that I was emotionally drained and had enough. I understood that my having an affair wasn't the right thing to do, but at that time, it was emotionally soothing and gratifying. I was becoming comfortable in the space that I was in and my husband and I were beginning to fight more often. The military police were frequently being called to do statements, once again it had become a common occurrence.

On February 14, 2004, while still in Europe, I was driving down the road with all four of our children and a very close friend when I spotted my husband who appeared to be walking hand-in-hand with another young lady. I had been calling him most of the day because he was supposed to be meeting me to spend the day with our kids so that I could get a breather. Although the speed limit was not very fast on the base, as I approached him, I could remember seeing red and jumped out of the driver seat, while the car was still moving! When I jumped out of the car, I began to get extremely loud and used profane language, which I'm certain embarrassed him in front of the young lady he was trying to impress. My husband and I yelled, pushed, and shoved all the way to the first set of apartments, which happened to be my best friend's apartment complex. It was approximately 2:00 pm in broad daylight with a large number of people outside watching us fight. My husband became so irate that he grabbed me by the front of my face, picked me up with one hand, and put my head through a windshield of a parked van, thus busting the windshield of the van. When I finally lifted my head, I was bleeding in the back of my head. My adrenaline was flowing, and my fight-or-flight instincts kicked in. I began to really fight back because at that time I felt as though he was prepared to hurt me, unlike before. He had an anger that I had never encountered.

My friend came downstairs with a knife, I grabbed the knife, and I was chasing him around the building with the knife, prepared to stab him, if I had been capable of making contact. The entire time, my children had been watching us. What were they learning? How did this entire interaction make them feel? I never asked. How was I shaping them as young adults? Was I concerned or had I even considered that? The answer was- NO! I wasn't considering my children and there was a price to pay.

This last occurrence should have been enough for me to wake up, but again, I thought I was smart enough to recognize the signs. I stayed with my husband and naturally, things progressed and as they say, things never get better. He continued his infidelities and I continued to feel even more insecure and lacking. I failed to understand that it wasn't really about me; my husband had his own issues that he needed to work on within himself.

One of our final incidents sent me to jail. I came home from working in Afghanistan to put the pieces together from yet another infidelity. I called my husband and told him that he had to come get all his things out of our home and leave. I had given him a few hours and would take the children to a movie to allow him time to do so. When I arrived back home, he had not packed anything. He made it clear that he was not leaving. I began to pack his things in a large black trash bag and started to throw them on the lawn. He became irate! An altercation ensued which resulted in him cutting up all of the furniture, busting up the 55-gallon fish tank, breaking all the glass in the home, bleaching up all my clothes, busting the windows to the front of the home and splashing spaghetti sauce on the walls of the home. I called the police and was told that there was nothing that they could do because the home was considered community property and that he could continue to damage the home in their presence, which he did. I became so irate that I threw my cell phone at him and was immediately arrested on a domestic violence charge. It was then and there when the reality officially hit me. This was all DOMESTIC VIOLENCE!! I was arrested in front of my children! I felt as though I had lost everything at that point; my freedom, my clearance, my job, my children, my entire livelihood.

I thought of all the years that I had personally endured physical trauma, and emotional abuse; in that moment I realized I wasn't as smart as I thought I was. I had not recognized the signs until the officers had charged me for throwing a cell phone. My children were in the home that night and had watched the entire occurrence unfold. They were crying and screaming. I had to call my parents to come to the home to pick them up. The entire time I was crying and asking myself, "How did I get here? How did I let things get this far? How did I not recognize the signs?" I knew I had seen them before.

I should have known how to recognize the signs; I should have been smarter. I had always sworn to be smarter than my mother. You see, as a child I watched my mother endure domestic violence. My father beat my mother what seemed like breakfast, lunch, and dinner, while my siblings and I watched. My childhood was dysfunctional and unhappy. I resented my mother and could not figure out why she stayed as long as she did and subjected us to the lifestyle that we experienced. My father was a habitual drug abuser, and we were a low-income family. When my father could not find enough money to get his next fix, he took his anger out on my mother who then took her anger out on predominantly me as the oldest of eight children. My father would sell absolutely everything in and around the home, from our furniture, the meat in the freezer, to our school clothes, among other things. So, when I asked myself, "How did I get here?" I wasn't asking because I didn't know, I'm just surprised that I wasn't as smart as I thought I was to remind myself that I had been brought up in this environment. I had created a mental block of my toxic childhood. I wanted to forget about the things that had happened to me as a child and move on with my life, not understanding that I had to deal with my past to heal for my future. I had been masking all those years and making excuses, not only for my mother and father, but now for my husband and for myself.

With God's grace, I found a new me and began to love myself again. I am remarried to a man who is patient and kind. I have acknowledged my history of domestic violence and done the work to heal. I had to realize that all the time that I thought I was sacrificing for the good of my children, to stay in an unhealthy marriage, I was actually hurting them. Each of my children are now adults and they have expressed what they went through from their perspective and how unhappy and stressed they were witnessing my abuse. I would be remiss not to mention that my father has been drug-free for more than 20+ years and that my parents have been married for more than 45+ years. However, not every relationship will be capable of standing the test of time.

I have had conversations with my daughters about domestic violence and having a zero-tolerance for mental, emotional or physical abuse. These are conversations that my mother never had with me. My mother's acceptance of her situation was a test of her faith, not of societal acceptance. My ex-husband and I are now in a good place. We have reconciled and have accepted the damage that we inflicted on each other; although there are still some things that he sees differently than the way I saw them. We both have grown in different ways. My ability to forgive, but not forget, allows me to release the baggage of my past so that I can move into a healthy and healed future. I may have been broken but I'm blessed!

If someone you know starts off by telling you that their significant other is only yelling, then it escalates to pushing and shoving or something more physical; please get them help. Often, individuals don't realize that they are being abused. The more comfortable and complacent an individual becomes, the more dangerous a situation can lead to. If you are reading my story and see yourself in any of my altercations or self-sabotage, seek help! Domestic violence will not go away and usually escalates. There is no age limit of when domestic violence starts or ends. If you don't have the courage to leave, seek support. Take action to save your life and the life of those you love. Remember, with God you are never alone!

How Her Story Relates to My Story:

_____

_____

_____

_____

_____

_____

_____

_____

_____

_____

_____

_____

How Her Story Relates to My Story:

_____

_____

_____

_____

_____

_____

_____

_____

_____

_____

_____

_____

Author Keairra A. Adams

Keairra A. Adams

Ms. Keairra A. Adams is a Non-profit Fundraising and Development professional. She is an active "busy-body" who embraces her beliefs of commitment to scholarship and service and implements these principles in her daily life.

Ms. Adams is an alumna of the Illustrious National Treasure - Morgan State University, the University of Maryland, and Arizona State University. She holds a dual Bachelor of Arts in Humanities and Biology, as well as a Master of Science in Family and Human Development. Her scholastic odyssey came with many proud and notable laurels, that include gaining membership into six honor societies: The National Society of Collegiate Scholars, The Honor Society of Phi Kappa Phi, Sigma Alpha Pi – The National Society of Leadership and Success, Alpha Sigma Lambda, The International Dean's List Society, and The Golden Key International Honour Society. completing her undergraduate degree with Cum Laude distinction – ranking in the top ten percentile in her class, and mastering her graduate studies with a 4.1 concluding GPA.

She is exceptionally engaged in the community - in many facets - and strives to promote full, enriched, and healthy lives for all. She has always been passionate about people, particularly women and children, and selflessly offers herself and her time to those in need. She is often heard giving words of encouragement and motivating others, sonorously proclaiming, "YOU CAN DO IT"! Ms. Adams is a native of the Washington Metropolitan Area, a proud member of Delta Sigma Theta Sorority, Inc., mother to Kayla, and dog-mom to Kingsley.

She dedicates this first work of authorship to the following "To my dream team. My family. My friends. The ones who celebrate me in every season and keep me going while wondering how in the world I do it. It's because of you all! Mommy (Mina), there is no one like you. I am, all that I am, because of you. You are my constant. To Grandma and my Sh'angels. And most importantly, to my Kayla. Greatness is ahead of and upon you, Little Sugar."

Her favorite scripture is Philippians 4:6 – "Don't worry about anything, instead, pray about everything. Tell God what you need and thank Him for all He has done".

$L.O.T.U.S$

Learning to Overcome Turbulence and Ultimately Succeed

I could write a book... I think I will. Well, a chapter - at least - to start.

My story is one of triumphant perseverance; of deconstruction and reconstruction. I'm vaguely transparent, but let's try to peel back these layers and allow the lotus to bloom.

Ever since I was a little girl, I've lived in this fairytale world in my head. I guess you could say it was my "safe space" where I felt comfortable and most protected. In my world, it was always sunshine and rainbows with a persistent pursuit of happiness; good things always happened and nothing ever went wrong. Conversely, because of that, it prevented me from seeing the world for what it really was and people for who and how they were, and I became inhibited. At some point, reality reared its ugly head and I had to live in it. This was much different than the world I had built in cognition.

Saying and writing this is probably an admission of how I'd allowed some things, people, and experiences to defeat me internally, while externally, I'd still tried to exhibit the persona of my fairytale world. I always envisioned life to be like in the movies, because they depicted something better than what reality had to offer. But then I realized that the movies weren't real; it was scripted and staged with actors who put on airs. When I was 17 years old, upon graduating high school, I had devised a five-year plan for my life's goals and accomplishments. The plan was to be revisited at age 22 when this timeframe had run its course. I was going to go off to college, do great in school and join different high-regarded organizations, meet a nice guy, graduate, get married, buy a house and car, have a baby, get a job, go off to medical school and begin my journey to become a doctor; all by the age of 22. You see, this planned path was normal for me – and expected of me – as I'd always been regarded as the "pedestal child" who was mature and wise beyond my years. I had always earned good grades, was involved in extra-curricular activities, often among the favorites of the teachers and school staff, and never ceased to dream big and reach beyond the stars; a self-proclaimed perfectionist and overachiever.

How many of you know that most times, *our plan* isn't God's plan? I did go to college, but that was a given. I did meet a guy. I did join some organizations on campus. I'd done the things that were inevitable, but the extension of my plan hadn't quite actualized at the time. Might I note that the *only thing* that had gone according to my extended plan was the birth of my daughter, at the age of 22. I'd like to call her "the blessing of Grandma's gift".

Yet somehow, at the age of 22, I found myself as a single mother who had still not yet graduated college; I wasn't on an ideal path and had put more time, energy, and focus into things that were not worth it and did not serve me well. But hey, lesson learned, right? I was doing the best I could with what I had and what I knew while trying to deal with my own internal feelings of pain, betrayal, and wrongdoing. In my senior year of college, I'd become a commuter student. One day, toward the end of the spring semester, I was sitting in my last class which was three hours long. I received a call from my mother, who had become the daily caretaker for my daughter while I attended classes. She was in a frantic panic and exclaimed that my daughter was having a difficult time breathing. It was clear that my daughter had experienced her first asthma attack. Lamentably, however, doctors would not diagnose her at that time because she was so young. The medical staff had informed me that she would have to experience that horrifying ordeal at least three times or reach the age of three before they could render a diagnosis of chronic asthma. As one would imagine, I was displeased with this new information.

It was at that moment that I decided that I couldn't do this anymore and I uprooted myself, in my senior year. With Mommy and Grandma's comforting blessings and affirmations, I withdrew from classes at that school and transferred so that I could be closer to home and have the flexibility of the hybrid model with in-person and online classes. They assured me that I would be alright and do just fine. I promised them that I would obtain my degree and walk across the stage with honors. I did just that!

Painfully, my Grandma transitioned the semester before I graduated. That hit me hard and it was apparent in my work. Gratefully, Grandma became my angel and kept her hand on me. Though some of my work suffered (to my standard), my grades did not, and on her birthday – just a few months after her ascension and one month before my graduation – I received my honors and was inducted into one of the most prestigious honor societies! Grandma made her presence known in subtle ways.

Nevertheless, I came out on top. I did better, in that one year, than I had done in my entire collegiate tenure. Gained membership in several honor societies, received awards, accolades, and scholarships from the university President and other "higher-ups", and ultimately graduated with honors as I had promised. Opportunities that I had not been afforded where I was prior, had suddenly come knocking at my door in droves. There's no mistaking that God knows what he's doing and it's all in His timing.

2016, whew! The first half of the year had everything looking up. But the second half... I'd just gotten approved for my new home and moved in. Secured a new job. I was just doing "big girl" things on my own and - in a sense - felt like I had grown up. Yeah, maybe I was feeling myself. Okay, okay, I WAS - perhaps a little too much - yet, not boastful about it, but humble.

God stripped me.

That new, good-paying job that I'd thought was my "come up" and a new beginning, I'd lost it just as fast as I'd settled in. I didn't work for nearly two years! No one knew. When I did, they were odd jobs; nothing secure. My vehicle was broken into, right in front of my garage. Home, on the line. My home was broken into, ransacked, and vandalized. Shortly after, I was in a car accident and totaled my SUV – the same one that had been burglarized less than a year prior. On top of it all, I was sick! I had no idea, nor did I realize how bad it was. I had no sense of security in any aspect of my life. I felt like an open wound that kept getting poked and sprinkled with salt. Wide-open. Unprotected. Vulnerable. Suppressed. Oppressed. De... You get it.

Anxious to do something good and cure myself of idleness, bad luck, and boredom, I decided to immerse myself in something with a fruitful outcome and began a graduate program. My darkness needed a glimmer of light. The year 2018 I brought about some high and lows, too. Just as I'd felt like I made it through and out of my storm and celebrated it, the overcast came and purged the second half of the year. It was not until 2019, that I was able to really begin my healing process. It was PERSONAL! A year of work, of grinding, of proving! Moreover, it was a year of finishing what I started and pursuing dreams that I started to think were unattainable. Surely there were universal elements putting the press on me, trying to stop everything! I could have died that year, TWICE. Near-death experiences really have a way of putting things into perspective. My health was restored, and that was MAJOR! Several appointments, what seemed like endless testing, multiple opinions from different doctors, "faking the funk", trying to show "the world" my best face and trying to convince myself that I was okay, yet knowing that I wasn't! I can't even describe how I felt but I kept myself busy to ignore it. I'd been sick for a very long time; at least three years and barely anyone knew. I was the woman with the issue of blood! Without any of the gruesome details, I ended up having surgery to correct the issue that had plagued me for so long. My blood count was so low, that the medical team was almost afraid to go through with the surgery. If my levels had dropped a mere two points below where they were, that table could have been the last place I'd ever laid my head. My God... Here I am!

I finally graduated with my Master's degree. I swear curveballs became a trend during this journey. I took a year longer than anticipated. I started; I became overwhelmed and discouraged and stopped. I laced up my sneakers and got back in the game!

Once I set my sights on a May 2019 graduation, the curveballs came in rapid-fire! I was told on about four occasions that I could not and would not graduate on time. "They" said it was impossible, "they" said it had never been done before, "they" said it was highly unlikely, but NONE of these things meant that it couldn't be done! At one point, I had a financial balance and therefore, couldn't register; TACKLED THAT. Then it was too late to register for a core class that I needed in order to graduate AND was only offered once a year; I JUMPED THAT HURDLE. Then, I was told that my capstone proposal might not be able to be reviewed in time and that my fieldwork experience wasn't going to work out, BUT IT DID. Then I received an email saying that I couldn't take two very challenging classes at the same time and in the very last semester; BODIED THAT! Tell me one thing... "Who gon' stop me, Boo?!"

So, I'd conquered all of the obstacles and made it to graduation. While in Arizona, I'd ventured off on my own to do a solo road trip and check one major thing off my bucket list. When I was done and had started on my way to return to where I was staying, darkness had fallen. I found myself on a lonely, dark, two-lane highway, in the "middle of nowhere/wilderness"; no streetlights and no other cars in sight, but the animal kingdom was VERY present. No, I wasn't lost - I was on the right and only road back to where I was going. Almost inevitable, I was in a single-car accident; spun three times, veered off the main road, hit a tree, and found myself pointing downward in a ditch, about a foot from a creek. I could hear the water rushing and the creatures "creatchin."

Let me pause right here and ask: have you ever seen an elk?! In real life!? Well, my accident was the result of trying to miss a family of elk darting to cross the street. It was me in the "toy car" versus three behemoth elk! Now you tell me who was going to win?! Not I! I sat down there for about two hours. Phone service was nearly nonexistent, and about three cars passed me before one kind young man realized that I was down there. As quirky as he was, he'd heard the faint sound of my horn, saw the car lights flashing and he thought to himself - "That's a weird way to park." Thankfully, he saw fit to be a good Samaritan and check it out. He helped me, called for police and a tow truck, and stayed with me until the authorities came.

Though shaken and exhausted, I made it to my graduation the next day! And while driving to the venue, I looked down at my wrist and the charm on my bracelet that was upright and facing me, read "Angels Watching Over Me". Yes, I'd also been wearing it the night before when that terrifying ordeal occurred. Grandma had made her presence known once again and let me know that she was with me. This moment, and the entire experience, was extremely emotional for me. I was on the brink of my breakthrough; I could feel it and I just knew it. All that I had gone through was coming to a head. I wept throughout the entire commencement ceremony. It was almost as if it were a cleansing and I was releasing all that I had carried for the last few years. Again, I say... HERE. I. AM!

I accomplished my goals. I survived the things I thought would have killed me. I finally embraced and claimed the changes in my life, my Saturn Return. Before that, I hadn't really let it resonate nor acknowledged that I'd experienced a major transition; a "coming of age".

I still experienced some losses that year, which were gut-punching and heart-wrenching. My support system lost a few pillars. They contributed to my being, my successes, and helped this young lady along the way. I've always felt like Grandma had her hands on them, to have their hands on me because they pushed me, poured into me, and celebrated me just as she would. My Sh'angels.

As I peaked in many facets of this evolution, I came across a shirt one day that spoke to me on levels that seemed so beyond this world. The front read "Girl Rising" and the back read "One girl with courage is a revolution". It was the only one of its kind and in my size. Undoubtedly, it was for me! This young lady who is often afraid of change and typically reluctant to push-back and self-advocate had somehow found the courage in every situation that came against her, and she rose. She is me.

Work Hard. Play Hard. Slay Hard. PRAY HARD.

If you've not ever witnessed the blossoming of a lotus flower, I encourage you to research it and view a video, preferably in time-lapse mode. Much like myself, the lotus begins in a tightly balled-up state; closed and shielded from the perils of the outside elements. It is slow and careful as it opens up and bares itself to the world, presenting its true beauty in the most modest way. As the day winds down, it retracts and retreats as a form of protection and self-preservation. I'm not the rose that grew from concrete, rather, the lotus in the murky waters. I guess it's safe to say, "I get it out the mud" and every time life pulls me under, I resurface, unscathed.

How Her Story Relates to My Story:

_____

_____

_____

_____

_____

_____

_____

_____

_____

_____

_____

_____

_____

How Her Story Relates to My Story:

_____

_____

_____

_____

_____

_____

_____

_____

_____

_____

_____

_____

_____

_____

Author Michelle Davis

Michelle Davis

Michelle Davis is a native of Alabama; however, she now calls Georgia home. She began her military career in June 1985 at Lackland Air Force Base, San Antonio, Texas for basic training and graduated from technical school as a Material Facilities Specialist at Lowery Air Force Base, in Colorado. After spending two years in the Alabama Air Force National Guard, Michelle joined the active-duty Army. Her first duty assignment was Baumholder Germany (The Rock). Michelle completed her military career on September 2015, at Shaw Air Force Base in South Carolina. She is married and the mother of three children, and grandmother to two grandchildren.

Michelle holds an associate degree in Business Administration, a bachelor's degree in Human Resource Management, and a master's degree in Organizational Leadership and Human Relations. She is currently pursuing her Doctorate.

Michelle considers herself a life-long learner. She admittedly acknowledges that she is flawed and has ghosts, demons, and traumas that affect her present. She hopes by sharing her story that the ghosts and demons will be not only released but banished forever and the physical and emotional trauma will be healed. This is her hope not only for herself but for all who are bound in plain sight.

Instructions NOT *Included*

Wife, Mother, Soldier, Daughter, Sister, and Friend all in one, however, instructions were not included. I was raised in the South by my mother and father and a small village of adults that checked you if you were wrong. My mother and father worked full-time and raised seven children and many neighborhood children. My mother was the epitome of a strong black woman. She taught me how to cook, clean, and sew, just to name a few things. My father gave me a love for reading; unlocking my imagination and showing me how I could travel anywhere in books. That knowledge is a *superpower* that cannot be taken from me. My military sergeants taught me how to be a good leader, put my soldiers first, how to breathe while calling cadence, and that I was not a girl but a soldier. All of these were great things to know. Yet no one taught me how to balance it all and not lose my mind, and most importantly myself.

I joined the Air Force Guard in protest at seventeen. It had been my desire to join the Army, but I needed the signatures of my parents and they were not hearing anything about the Army. After two years in the Air Force, I fulfilled my goal and joined the Army. Within a year of joining the Army, I was pregnant with my first child. At three years, I was married which added another child to the mix, and pregnant with a third child. I had achieved promotions and now was a responsible for the welfare of other soldiers. My day started at 4 a.m. and ended at 12 a.m. and as the years went on the space between that 4 and 12 would get closer and closer.

I often found myself in situations where I was the only female in the group. Which meant I was also the only mother and wife in the group. There were no special considerations for daycare or for me getting dinner on the table for my family; my requirements were the same as the males I stood beside. Soldier and Mom in that order as far as my Supervisors were concerned.

I was in Baumholder, Germany, on the post's Powerlifting Team, living what I considered at the time, as my best life. I went to the doctor because I was not feeling well. The doctor said, "You are pregnant." I was in extreme denial and apparently so was my first sergeant and my supervisors. At five months pregnant, I found myself in the field face down in the mud after falling off a 5-ton truck in Wildflecken, Germany. After the fall, the doctor recommended that I be returned to the home station for bed rest. The Commander and First Sergeant were not having any of that; they instead opted for me to sleep on a cot in a tent for the remainder of the field exercise. The rest of my pregnancy would continue with more of the same; my pregnancy was no excuse for not pulling my load. I would remain working in the motor pool with all the fumes and all the trucks until my seventh month of pregnancy. At seven months, I was moved to the supply room; this would be my only good fortune during my pregnancy.

On June 6, 1989, at 10:45 a.m. at Landstuhl Hospital in Germany, I gave birth to a beautiful baby girl. There was no one in the delivery room holding my hand, telling me when to push, and that I could do this. This delivery was a solo job. On June 9th I took my daughter home to a flat no bigger than a very small bedroom. No one was there to greet us because my daughter's father had returned to Chicago to marry the mother of his first child on the very day I brought our daughter home. He had done so with a conflicted soul and at the time I did not press the issue. I never wanted to marry someone just because I had a child by them. I had resolved that I was alone and found solace in a song by Cheryl Pepsii Riley called "Thanks for my Child". Twenty-four hours after bringing my daughter home I would find myself back in the hospital with complications from childbirth and my daughter would have to stay with a soldier in my unit for the first week of her life.

After six weeks of convalescent leave, I returned to work. On my first day back, still bleeding from childbirth, we did a 12-mile ruck march. My Squad Leader and Platoon Sergeant were determined to break me and make me get out of the army. By the time we finished the ruck march that day my uniform was soaked in blood my body was aching all over and I felt defeated. That night I prayed and cried, cried and prayed. I felt there was no way I was going to be able to remain in the army and take care of my baby. I felt like God was truly punishing me and I thought I deserved it. While sobbing I remembered a bible verse; "For his anger endureth but a moment, and in his favor is life; weeping may endure for the night, but joy cometh in the morning." (Psalm 30:5 KJV) I convinced myself that I could do this; I could figure this Motherhood and Soldiering thing out. I tried for many months to balance it all. I had no car and I lived five miles from my babysitter. Every morning rain, sleet, or snow, I would bundle my baby up and walk her to the babysitter. I would then run two miles to work to do physical fitness training (PT) with my unit. I was so tired I often fell out of the company runs which meant after PT, I would have *remedial* PT.

I could barely pay my rent and feed myself; there were no WIC or food stamps for soldiers in Germany. Towards the end of my tour in Germany, I found myself still struggling. So, with a heavy heart, I took my daughter home to my mother. I returned to Germany to finish out my tour, moving back in the barracks where I endured late-night room inspections by my drunken Squad Leader that included unwanted fondling. I often had to block the door for protection. A few months later, I would clear my installation and prepare to move back stateside. One of the squad leaders in my platoon volunteered to take me to the airport. I thought nothing of this because of all the Non-Commissioned Officers in the unit this NCO was a godly man who seemingly went to church every day. I had no reason to think that I would be anything other than safe with him. I was grateful for the ride to the airport. Upon arriving at the airport, the sergeant walked me to the gate, and in what still seems like a nightmare he grabbed me, groping my breasts and buttocks. He pulled me so violently into him the air left my body. He then kissed me so hard my jaws popped. No one in the airport even flinched. With tears rolling down my face I walk down the corridor found my seat and sobbed in silence.

My joy would still come in the morning because I would be reunited with my daughter. The reunion proved to be emotionally, physically, and financially draining. My mother had taken great care of my daughter. She had fallen in love with my daughter and did not want me to take her with me. The exchange ended with my mother striking me so hard that I fell against the car. The blow was worth it to have my daughter back with me. I was stationed just 45 miles away. I was stateside and yet I found myself still struggling to support myself and my daughter. I moved into a small furnished apartment which was often broken into. I was not far from my hometown, but I was still struggling financially. I was still seeing my daughter's father (now a married man) but I was not receiving financial support. Now stateside, he was continuing to live his best life.

Many of my friends that found themselves struggling had given up custody of their children to their relatives. But I was determined to raise my daughter myself. I did things during that period that I am not proud of, but for my daughter, I would do it all again. I was surviving by any means necessary.

Just when I started to see light at the end of the tunnel, it was time to deploy to Desert Storm. I would once again have to rely upon someone else to take care of my daughter. Her father and I had worked through some of our issues. He would look after her briefly and then take her to his mother because he was also deploying to the Middle East.

After my deployment, I moved into on-post housing. I had no furniture, and no pictures for the walls, but I had this amazing little girl. I remember going to the furniture store to buy furniture and discovering what a credit score was and simultaneously discovering that I had very bad credit. My mother had put furniture in my name at the local furniture store which would not have been a problem if those bills were paid with the money that was being sent home. So, there I was, home from deployment and before I could get started, I had bad credit and immense debt. The rub of it all was that in the military if you accumulate too much debt, you lose your clearance which in turn gets you kicked out. So, there I was again face down in the mud, but this time was different: defeat became determination. If I could stand up once with nothing but the grace of God, I could stand up again.

Now, the challenge was to balance it all. I couldn't afford luxuries. I told my daughter that carrots were candy and she bought it. I made a game out of the empty house. My daughter could scream and hear her voice echo which made her laugh. I made a pallet on the floor from clothes and a sheet. I bought a used sewing machine from Goodwill and took old dresses and made jumpers for my daughter. I used cloth diapers. I made curtains out of sheets and pictures for the wall out of pages from magazines. I folded contact paper into fans and tacked them on the walls. I eventually convinced a sales agent at Farmers Furniture to sell me a couch and a love seat. He overcharged me, but I was grateful to have somewhere to sit.

Things with my daughter's father were still rocky, yet we got married after I became pregnant with our son. He had followed through on the divorce and mailed me a copy while we were deployed. Our first act together would be to empty our savings account and pay off the furniture my mother had put in my name while I was deployed. So, we drove to my hometown and in his front yard, counted out two thousand dollars in the hand of the owner of the furniture store. It was now time to go to our next duty station.

I returned to Germany where I struggled with what I now know was PTSD. I would travel to Germany alone, four months pregnant, to set up our living quarters. I arrived in Germany after sleeping most of the journey, to awake soaked in blood. I was rushed to the hospital where the doctors informed me that I had had a spontaneous miscarriage of one of my twins. I was scared, devastated, and alone but I had to push through and take care of the business at hand. A few weeks later my husband and daughter arrived. We welcomed our son on July 12,1992. Like his sister, setting eyes on him almost burst my heart with joy.

The next 30 years would be full speed ahead filled with the good, bad, and sometimes ugly. Nothing in our lives would happen like it did on television or in the books I had read. I missed birthdays anniversary and even funerals. I struggled with being a Soldier Wife and Mother. I struggled with having a healthy relationship with my Mom, my siblings and myself. I was afraid of failing my Children, my Husband my Family and my Soldiers. I was afraid to saying "no" and said "yes" way too much.

Somethings I put in place in my life. Prior to deployment, I celebrate birthdays early with my children. I found that Christmas and Thanksgiving can be on any day of the year. Valentine's Day should be as often as you think of it and never on February 14th. We raised our three children as sisters and brother they are NOT stepsisters and stepbrother. Friday night in our house became family night. We created" No Contact Day"; all cell phones turned off, no disturbance from the outside. On that day, each member of the family can either stay in bed in their pajamas all day, eat what they want, and do what they want, as long as they do it at home. By the end of the day, we usually ended up all in one room, playing board games. I placed my children first.

There is no written set of instructions that will fit everybody and show you how to balance it all or how to survive every event in your life, but I offer you this: Be your best YOU every day. However, remember sometimes your best you may not be able to get off the couch, and that's okay. I tell Myself every day, "Alright Michelle, today you are going to do your best you." At the end of the day, I ask myself, "Did you do your best?" If my answer is "yes", I get a "well done". If it is "no", I immediately ask God for another chance to try again. The next day I wake in joy because God has granted me a do-over. My life instructions were clear as soon as I realized that my life's playbook is tailored-made for me. Trying to live by someone else's playbook does not work for me. Failure does not mean you are unsuccessful. My balance came only when I allowed somethings to fall. I have redefined my "noes" they now bring me Numerous Opportunities.

I am now retired after thirty years of honorable service. Our children are grown and our oldest has given us two beautiful grandchildren that bring us continued joy. My Parents are resting in Heaven. I strive every day to be a better person than I was yesterday. I don't know how my story ends or what I want to be when I grow up. I do know that I want to continue to grow and be present in every moment.

How Her Story Relates to My Story:

_____

_____

_____

_____

_____

_____

_____

_____

_____

_____

_____

_____

How Her Story Relates to My Story:

_____

_____

_____

_____

_____

_____

_____

_____

_____

_____

_____

Author Michelle Dowleyne

Michelle Dowleyne

Michelle Dowleyne is a motivational speaker, bestselling author, founder of a 501c3 nonprofit organization *Boots 2 Heels, Inc.* and Visionary of *Her Story is My Story*. She enjoys reading, spending time with her family, and relaxing. Michelle is currently married to Daryl Dowleyne. Together, they have a blended family of: two daughters, one son, one grandson, and one granddaughter.

She received her Bachelor's Degree in Psychology from Cameron University. She received her Master's Degree in Business Administration from Strayer University and she graduated with honors.

In March 2012, Michelle was diagnosed with Major Depression and Post Traumatic Stress Disorder. Despite these disabilities, she follows the lead of God and serves women by empowering them through her ministry. Her vision came to fusion in March 2020 during the pandemic. As a result of her own personal struggles, she derived her drive for helping others and this has become her passion. If she can help one person by sharing her story, then the healing process begins because she understands that HER story is MY story. She believes her disability is not a setback but a blessing that enables her to help others seek self- awareness and empowerment.

Michelle loves God and believes He guides her path. Being actively involved in her community, she spends a lot of time volunteering. She believes that we live in communities where we can see the development of more powerful and successful women being a resource to each other and to the community instead of being a liability. Michele reminds us to- *"Believe in yourself and all that you are. Know that there is something inside you that is greater than any obstacle."* Christian D. Larson

Contact Compilation Visionary At:
Website: *www.michelledowleyne.com*
Email: *AuthorMichelleDowleyne@gmail.com*
Facebook: *Facebook.com/groups/HerStoryIsMyStory/*

The Visionary Unmasked

I am the Visionary of *Her Story is My Story,* founded to help women seek self-awareness, motivation, and empowerment. I seek to inspire women to see the worth inside them and not depend on others to set their worth. In March 2012, I was diagnosed with Major Depression; yes, I struggle with depression. I also struggled with how God had chosen to use me as a vessel. I didn't understand how God gives me the vision or strength to empower others when there are days I can't get out of bed. One thing I do know is that where he leads me, I most unquestionably will let him guide me.

Some people ultimately have a period in life when they are stuck. A period when our life is a life equal to mere existence when you do not know why you wake up, or what you want each day when nothing makes you happy. If you do not know what this feeling is like, you have been a happy person and lived a blessed life.

Depression is not temporary boredom or being in a bad mood. Depression is often a long and challenging process. Insomnia, restlessness, aggression, anger, loss of sense of security, despair when you think there is no other way, nothing to change for the better, loss of energy and concentration, difficulty communicating with people, and feelings of loneliness. You see me, but you don't see ME because this is the true me. I am the summation of this list of symptoms.

Let's take a stroll down memory lane. I don't want you all to get too comfortable in wanting to be like the visionary. "You see me, but you don't see ME." Sometimes being a leader, visionary, or anyone with a passion for helping others, a price comes with the shine. On the outside, people see the shine, the hustle, the smiles, and connections. But what they don't see is the restless nights, days of not eating, feeling like life will never bring you joy. Why, because we put on a mask so that others can't see the true us. I used to get headaches when it was time for me to go out because I didn't want to be around people. I kept a calendar and knew my schedule because I knew that anything out of the ordinary would cause stress and anxiety. As the time got near for me to get ready to go out, my anxiety kicked in. I would lose my keys, couldn't focus, and I began to get sick. I spent days on top of days in the bed, not wanting or thinking about getting out of the bed. I would only get up and show up when absolutely needed.

My husband would have to drive me everywhere. He did the cooking, and grocery shopping because I would say I didn't like going out. It still seems strange to me to divulge this: the signs started once I retired. I couldn't tell anyone because I was embarrassed by what people would think. This go-getter, high performer, and to some, the lady who has it all together has depression???? Would my value or perception of whom they thought I was, go down? Would people stop asking me to be a part of projects, take leads, or would they now see me as someone seeking pity? So, I did what I thought would not embarrass my family or me and hide the fact that I had depression.

Of course, it would get worse because surely, I would have to take medication. That journey confirmed that the world was a scary place, and I could not survive in it. That hurt me; I was ashamed. I helped people pass through this point, but why couldn't I seem to help myself. All these fears that I tried to avoid daily were part of a pattern that convinced me that they were irrefutable facts. It doesn't matter if everyone around me (my friends, my family, my doctors) told me that they will always support me or that I was not alone. Depression and my PTSD convinced me, more than once, more than twice, that life would never be the same, and I understood that. It was suggested that I take antidepressants, and I didn't even understand that needing a drug meant that this was a treatable disorder, at the time. It was recommended to me by a doctor, and I answered, outright, that I would not take them. No, why not.

I didn't tell him that I thought it was *terrible* for me to be prescribed an antidepressant; it frightened me. In my world, as a strong female and African American, you didn't take medication, and you surely didn't seek a psychiatrist. Again, I convinced myself. I think that the drive for self-improvement, in the world in which we live, deceives us all the time.

In any case, the doctor told me that these medicines had to be accompanied by a therapeutic process to help me gain control of my feelings. For example, I had to learn to not always stay inside and be aware of the obsessive ways that I approached situations. For example, sabotaging projects that in other circumstances gave me satisfaction or a *sense of purpose.*

I had been a speaker for years, sharing that these disorders, yes, disorders, do not define me but created a new me. I have written several books elaborating on my depression, PTSD, and its causes. But today, I share about my drive to live and manage my disorders because I understand life is worth living. I'm feeling the same way as many others in America because, **Her Story is My Story.** We must share our story to give hope to others who may be facing the same challenges.

For years, I felt that every act I wanted to perform was met by resistance from my body, resistance from my mind: disinterest, fatigue, silence, sadness. All that lives and twists, still, in my head. I wonder what the lady who struggles to get out of bed would think if she knew that the lady she looks up to as a mentor also struggles with depression. I wonder no more because I choose to tell my story. I prefer to share for those who feel embarrassed to let others know that they are high achievers, but there are days on top of days they are lying in bed hopeless. As women, we are born to be everyone's all and all. We take on every role there is in a household except self-provider. Women will live with depression, highs, and lows and still show up for everyone else except for themselves. It's time to take control of our life and live. You are worth so much and have a vital role in the family, society, and our community. They don't say- "behind every man is a strong woman" for no reason. It's not a cliche; it is the truth. Ladies, we are stronger than we think. I am here to tell you to believe in yourself. Put as much energy as you give others into yourself. Like a flower, you will blossom if you have faith.

Depression and PTSD work that way in me: Ups and downs make me determined to help other women, but I can't help myself from experiencing this feeling. I did not, nor ever attempted to do myself physical harm. Cause at this time, it has been a "pure mental process". We confront this issue head-on, Therefore, let's say: "Today, from here, I will not leave." Between my eyes and my mind, I had something like a smokescreen made of fear, fatigue, sadness, and that curtain pressed on my nerves; it was going to come out of my eyes. But no, not anymore. After years of fighting this terrible battle, I rise to say I am a conqueror!

One morning I managed to sit in front of the computer. I tried to write an article on self-worth for one of my upcoming speaking engagements. It was then that I came across another surprising fact; no matter how hard my brain tried to command my hands to put one word after another, nothing happened. My hands didn't react; my brain was blank. I tried to think of what to type, but suddenly I didn't even understand the topic on which I was supposed to write. I had already been preaching this content to other women. I knew this topic oh so well.

I was sitting there with a blank stare when my husband walked in. "What wrong?" he asked. I answered what I could: "I don't know, I don't know. I cannot anymore. I can't help people deal with their depression, and I struggle with my depression." Why was I chosen to do this? God said He wouldn't put more on you than you can bear, but clearly, he is with me, I thought.

I had let myself fall; it was my fault that I had allowed myself to *weaken* in that way, and therefore I couldn't push anymore. What was I going to do? So many women and women veterans had depended on me. I came out with a bang, and now I can't produce. BUT, when God is in the head of your life, He gives you the strength to do what His plans are in your life.

111

I live trying not to be like that, not to let sadness put me against the wall and exhaust me. I live trying not to stumble upon obstacles such as long-lasting crying for hours, for no apparent reason; trying not to convince myself that I am a perpetual and irreparable failure, depression got me used to thinking like that. It's still hard for me to say: it's not my fault that I feel this way; I guess going through depression helps me know how to empower the other women because I know what they are going through; self-doubt, self-worth, and so on. Depression is not just a disease of how the mind and emotions operate; it is also physical. It is also personal and can happen to anyone even if we do not understand precisely why.

A person who hides his or her PTSD can do so in destructively creative ways. I can put in too much overtime at my visionary work to ignore the axioms of PTSD that my mind repeatedly chants, like "you don't deserve to be where you are."

In my visionary work, with God's help, I can automate my actions by feeling involved with those I am seeking to help. I can connect with them on many levels because I understand how they are feeling. Being automatic in my response is not healthy. The truth only postpones what I ignore.

So, when I must take action to take care of myself at the expense of the world around me stopping functioning (as if that were true), I feel guilty. God was telling me that my life wasn't *bad enough* for me to be feeling this bad. I was doing what I've always wanted to do; I dedicate myself to my visionary work; I live, in general, without major material setbacks, without debts. I live with my husband within reach of a call, and with a great support group.

And I, even at this point, still convince myself that I will not be able to change how I live this constant malaise. This self-sabotage and prejudice did a lot to make my disbelief of hope for recovery a part of my personality. Between doctors, my husband, and friends rally in agreement. They have consistently tried to convince me that *my thing* is I seek to eradicate shame, I self-sabotage, and I suffer from guilt. Acceptance and self-awareness guides me in understanding myself. The sadness is still there, at times, but I try to maintain the discipline of always informing myself. Many communicators talk about their depression in the medium they work in, knowing that it is necessary to talk about it in public.

Getting informed implies facing reflections on how we who suffer from this type of disorder can cope with the symptoms and how we can separate ourselves from them. Sometimes I find interview nuggets like this: "When a disease does not kill us but is chronic, it is essential that we understand it as an inner part of our life story, as part of ourselves and not like an alien force."

How Her Story Relates to My Story:

_____

_____

_____

_____

_____

_____

_____

_____

_____

_____

_____

_____

How Her Story Relates to My Story:

_____

_____

_____

_____

_____

_____

_____

_____

_____

_____

_____

_____

_____

Author Nicole Dunn

Nicole Dunn

Nicole was born and raised in Camden, New Jersey, and has been residing in Maryland for the last eighteen years. She is currently married with a blended family: together they have three sons, one daughter, and one grandson.

She received her Bachelor of Science in Business Administration with a major in Computer Information Systems from Hawaii Pacific University. Nicole received her Master of Science in Information System Security degree from Strayer University.

She served her country at numerous locations throughout the United States and abroad, including supporting Operation Enduring Freedom and Operation Iraqi Freedom. In April 2008, she returned from a deployment, only to hear that her life would never be the same. Diagnosed with Post Traumatic Stress Disorder (PTSD) Nicole was informed that it could be managed with medications and therapy because Post Traumatic Stress Disorders is something that many live with every day. She found it very difficult to manage her frequent emotional highs and lows and the demands of military life. She realized that something had to be done. She often told herself, "if you can hang in there for just four more years, you can retire." After 20 years of service to the U.S. Army, Nicole decided it was time for a change of scenery and she retired.

Nicole is an advocate of giving back to the community. She is associated with many organizations that focus solely on community involvement. Nicole is currently the Commander of her chapter of the Disabled American Veterans, where she wholeheartedly believes that every veteran has a *WHY* to motivate them to live.

She joined in with the visionary of *HER Story Is My Story* (HSIMS) to openly share "Her Story" in hopes of inspiring others to find their WHY!

Finding My Why

According to Friedrich Wilhelm Nietzche, "He who has a *WHY* to live can bear almost any *HOW*." At the age of 45, I was craving something in life that I could not quite identify. Where on my journey in life, did I lose it? What was it? If I didn't know what it was, how could I fix it? Ultimately, I wanted to know- what do I need to do to be that happy outgoing me.

I took a stroll down memory lane. In high school, I joined a lot of organizations to stay active and out of the house. My senior year was midway through, yet I had no roadmap that I felt was achievable. My family's history of success blocked my thinking. It wasn't until I was at a best friend's house for an overnight stay that I had that life-changing conversation. As her mother and I talked about how the senior year was quickly coming to an end, she wanted to hear my plan. I nonchalantly stated, "I'm going to find a better job." Immediately she responded, "Nik you're going to college"; as if saying a job was not enough. My best friend's mother then repeated her declaration with more emphasis-" Oh, you are going to to college!" The force of her words was so impactful that I felt a noticeable chill run through my body, the type you feel when you're in church and you're praising and worshiping, yes, that type. At that very moment, my spirit was touched in a way that clearly said, despite your lack of financial stability, God will make a way! I fought to hold back the tears as I managed to force a smirk onto my face. I immediately walked to the bathroom to relieve the tears that were swelling up in my eyes. As I looked in the mirror, I told myself, "You have excellent grades, you know what you would like to do, go for it!" If I wanted to change the course of my family, it was time to make a decision to move forward, starting with me. This is one of the first encounters when I realized I have found my *WHY* to live but didn't know *How* I was going to accomplish it.

Looking back, I realized, I often navigated and held close to other girls my age that had and were doing things that I only wished I had or could do with my family. My senses continuously grew keen about my future and where and what I wanted to be. While I was never ashamed of my family, I often asked myself- "Why don't I want to mimic anything that they do?" It was not for a lack of their being, but more so a lack of their motivation to move forward. They were all happy, just living. For some reason, that was not enough for me. I must say, I was wealthy with love from my family. My grandmother had thirteen children. Therefore, in addition to parents and siblings, there were aunts, uncles, and cousins aplenty and we learned to lean on one another.

My best friend's mother's declaration was accurate. I did attend college and I hit the journey called life as I knew it. Things were going great. I finished up my second year of college at what was then, Trenton State College in New Jersey, only to learn that the grant I had was not enough to go back the following year. Immediately panic mode set it. The question that kept me up all night was- how are you going to get out of this situation. As friends discussed roommates for the next year, I kept quiet. That's me, play it like everything's cool. No one needs to know. I recall going to bed with the pit of my stomach in pain from stressing about finding the required money. I reached out to my father, only to be told every excuse in the book as to why he didn't have the money. The next morning, I took my last three dollars and caught the bus downtown to the U.S. Air Force recruitment office.

When I arrived, they were closed. Boy, were my feelings hurt. Well, I thought, "Let me check in with the U.S. Army recruiters." I was welcomed with a huge -" Hello, how can I help?" I kindly replied, "Do you know what time the Air Force recruiters will be there?" "We're not sure, he responded, but maybe I can answer your questions." Little did I know his invitation would lead me to enlist into the Army! To top it off, the recruiter had to give me a ride home because I didn't have enough money for the bus! In other situations, like this, I tended to suppress my feelings until they push me to act. I'd developed the mentality to sustain and maintain on my own. No looking back.

My military career was going great. I completed my bachelor's degree; my son was in every sport I could sign him up for; I was loving life at church, serving as an usher and on top of that, I was asked to be the junior usher's supervisor/mentor. What more could I want or need. I was volunteering a couple of times every week: anything that I could do to give back to the community was my focus. I now had enough money to help my mother and relatives back home. Life was grand, as I knew it. I now realize that during this phase of my life I was acting out of my hidden feelings. Providing for others provided me the satisfaction that I had wanted to receive when I was journeying through the earlier years of my life. I felt that my WHY or purpose in life was to give of my time, talents, and money (the little that I saved) to help others the same way that I desired to be helped.

Time moved swiftly; my son was turning nine when I was informed; it's time to deploy to Iraq. "No worries, I thought, I'm strong, and I can handle it." Little did I know that deployment was a little more than my mental abilities could handle. A *day* in Iraq was like working in an office back home. However, the nights were a different story. What I prayed so reverently would not happen while I was stationed in Iraq, happened. During the nights, we were in a war zone, taking direct fire! This occurred off and on during the first four months that I was in Iraq. Then the frequency and intensity of the direct attacks increased! These life-threatening situations kept me on high alert and heightened my awareness. Well, that's what I called it at that time to cope and convince myself that I was still okay. After a year, I returned from Iraq, but I was not okay. More days and nights, I found myself waking with tingling and numbness in my hands and feet. I often blacked out at almost any sound that startled me. It wasn't until the day I was at work and a mild earthquake hit Maryland, that I woke up to people surrounding me asking- "Do you know who you are? Who am I?" I responded- "Why are y'all in my face and why am I on the floor?" It was that day that my doctor said, "Enough is enough, I'm taking you to Mental Health; you have Post Traumatic Stress Disorder (PTSD)."

PTSD is a mental health condition that's triggered by terrifying events that are either experienced or witnessed. Symptoms may include flashbacks, nightmares, and severe anxiety. Being the strong, persistent person that I was, I declared- "I will beat this in no time. Just tell me what I need to do; too easy." However, my symptoms got worse and began to interfere with my day-to-day life. I was at a point where my son could no longer walk in the room without startling me to a point that I would scream- "Can you let me know when you are coming into the room? That scared the mess out of me!" Enough was enough, this meant that the stack of medications I was prescribed; I had to start taking them. Visits to the psychologist and psychiatrist became more frequent. Still, I was not convinced that I was not normal.

It's Monday morning, doctor's visit today and the first thing that came to mind was- "Here I go again, and he wants to increase my medication. Is he serious?" The more I thought about it, the more I was reluctant to visit the doctor. I would leave my office, hours before my appointment, only to arrive at the psychiatrist's office just minutes before my appointment, and I had to conjure up the courage to go inside. Looking back, it wasn't courage that I needed to help move me from the comfort of my car, to go inside, it was the acceptance of the fact that I actually was going inside to seek the assistance of someone *else* to help me with my problems. This also meant that I would be admitting that I had a problem that I could not fix myself. Then *WHY* am I so involved with others' problems and issues? It wasn't just because I liked to hear, "I can't thank you enough or how can I ever repay you?" Satisfaction came just from seeing a sigh of relief on the person's face or hearing it in their voice. You know, it's the feeling you get after you have just eaten your favorite dish? Yes, their appreciation would leave me gleaming inside; just like a child that was left unsupervised in the candy store. So, after I spent 45 minutes to an hour sobbing, wiping snot from my nose, tears from my eyes, I would say- "Get it together! Go in there and act like you have it together!" Why shouldn't I? I had just paid

$50 to get my lashes done, $40 for my nails, picked out one of the best suits I had in my closet (Army fatigues) and by the way, I was carrying a new designer bag! There was no way, he or anyone else would ever know that I only slept two hours a night: tossing, turning, wondering if I would die in my sleep from an anxiety attack or if it was safe that I only took the medications on days I felt really bad. My *WHY* or rationale to live was now held on by a string; it was because of my son. How I was going get through this PTSD was a daily challenge.

It's so amazing how through tough times I would provide support to other people; helping them with their situations, but I felt that my situation was not relevant or important enough to be expressed. Impoverishment never kept me from pursuing my goals once they were set. I often thought- "Why am I allowing emotions to hold me back?"

Therapy helped me strengthen my *WHY*; helped break the deadlock; the deadlock that held my feelings towards myself hostage. I was feeling numb, no satisfaction for anything that I accomplished for myself, and I used my son as the only reason to live, to exist. In 2012, after four years, I could see and feel my *WHY* again!

It wasn't until my cousin was murdered in 2014. Once again, I felt as life itself was taken from me: as if someone had just put a device over my nose and mouth and sucked the breath right out of my body. To this day, if I ponder too long on his tragedy, I become numb all over again. He was my only hope of another family member helping to influence others to move forward, to live for a purpose. I had to find a purpose in life that was meaningful enough to me, to see me through. My PTSD and anxiety symptoms increased again. WHY? I thought I was fully recovered until I was told PTSD can live with you for years only to be triggered by new life events! Here I go, back on medications and in therapy. I had to accept that my *WHY* in life changes based on my circumstances. How did I find my *WHY*? My feelings were always based on my thoughts. Therefore, I changed my behavior based solely on this. Through continuous therapy, I learned that I had to look at situations differently and walk myself through them, step by step. I would then challenge myself to ask questions that were contrary to negative thoughts. I trained myself to focus on the positive aspects of any situation.

I now understand that it's important to be selfish for yourself. Selfish when deciding to take care of my invisible wounds. Do you know, it was a sigh of relief when someone presented me with their problem. On the other hand, it was a challenge if it was my own problem, issue, or situation. Helping others was my prime opportunity to stop thinking about myself and what I was struggling with at the time. Yes, time to do what I deemed as most important, and that was to help them resolve their problem.

Even today, I giggle to myself and say, my *WHY* will change, only because of my purpose to live! Day-to-day I anxiously wait for someone to ask WHY? Why do you do the things that you do? I will tell them- "It's because it helps heal my invisible wounds that I've carried since a child and throughout my adult life." It wasn't until I read the quote, "Success comes when we wake up every day in that never-ending pursuit of *WHY* we do what we do." – Simon Sinek. This quote also helps bring things into perspective in my life and enables me to accept that it's okay if my *WHY* changes. I never imagined that I would share my story. The realization came, that I too, could help aid someone, if only one, to find their WHY – Winsome, Holistic, You!

How Her Story Relates to My Story:

How Her Story Relates to My Story:

_____

_____

_____

_____

_____

_____

_____

_____

_____

_____

_____

_____

Author Pamela Keys

Pamela Keys

Pamela Sanders Keys was born in Winona, Mississippi, and has been residing in McDonough and Stockbridge, Georgia area since 2007. Pamela is married to George Keys and they have one daughter, Shante' Alston.

Pamela served 29 years in the United States Army, where she earned her Master of Business Administration degree. Pamela always had an interest in working with the youth. During her time in the military, she volunteered to work with the youth at the church and in the neighborhood. She has been a JROTC Instructor with Atlanta Public Schools for the past 10 and a half years.

Pamela not only has a passion for the youth, but she also has a passion for senior citizens. While she was in the military, she and her daughter often *adopted* elders who were in the nursing home. They committed to spend quality time with them. In 2010, Pamela started a nonprofit organization, *Connecting Winona Inc.* in her hometown to give back to the senior citizens in the community and nursing homes, and to the youth. Using her leadership skills, she was able to motivate her sisters, a high school classmate, people in her hometown, and some of her military friends to become actively involved in the organization.

Pamela loves the Lord and knows that if it was not for His grace and mercy she would not be here. She is on an assignment to touch as many people as possible in her community with the blessing that God has given her. She has a heart to serve.

From Project to Praise!

I grew up in the Projects, in a four-bedroom duplex with one bathroom and with eleven people (my Mom, sister, brother, my Aunt, and cousins). I learned at an early age that it was not just your Mom and Aunt raising you, but it was the community. If a grownup told you to do something, you did it and didn't question the adult. If you did, she would give you a "whooping" and you would get another one when you got home. This was just one of the values and standards that my mother taught us, and they are still with me today. Looking at families today, it is almost unheard of two black families living together. In addition, there has been a decline in the teaching of values and standards.

When I was five years old, my mother was told by her doctor that she could no longer work because she had a heart condition. I remember my mother getting food stamps (today it is the EBT card) and she would go someplace to pick up peanut butter, beans, powdered eggs, and cheese. When I was a kid, I had no idea that we were considered poor. I didn't know what staying in the Projects really meant. I knew my mother didn't have money to take my sibling and me shopping often. We would get things on special occasions and that taught me to take care of my things.

Growing up, my family went to church and attended Sunday School. Our church was about nine miles from our house, and although we had Sunday School every Sunday, we only had service once a month. My family church, Columbiana United Methodist Church was in the country. Bethlehem United Methodist Church was a couple of blocks from our house so we would attend Sunday school and sometimes church service there. One Sunday when I was eight years old, we were attending service at Bethlehem United Methodist Church. I remember crying, and this teenager named Ann

Marie Purnell asked me what was wrong. I replied- "The preacher is preaching too hard." Something had come over me and I could not explain it! Now I know it was the Holy Spirit. I can still remember being at my church and the choir singing without any music, just the stomping of their feet and feeling the spirit. I have been all over the world and I never experienced any choir that could sing like my home church choir.

At the age of eleven, our school. J. J. Knox burned down, and everyone was saying that it was arson. During that time, the government had just passed a law for the schools to be integrated and our school, the former all-black school was in our neighborhood, about two blocks from where I lived. It was a sad night. We were all out looking at the building burn and you would have thought the fire department could have saved half of the building, but they did not. The only thing that was saved was the gym and today, it is still being used for all middle and high school basketball games. At the age of 12, when I finished the school year, my mother sent me to Detroit to spend the summer with my Aunt and Uncle and their daughters. While I was there, I got my first job; it was at an ice cream shop and record store. I saved my money so when I went back home after the summer, I could buy my school clothes. I was so grateful the owners agreed to hire me every summer.

During my middle school years, I attended school in trailers on the foundation where J. J. Knox was. I had a math teacher named Mr. Jimmy Jones. I thought he was so cool; I never saw him raise his voice or get upset with anyone. One day during lunch, I saw him walking and I joined him and began to have a conservation with him. He asked me, "What do you want to do with your life after high school?" I replied, "I'm not sure." He told me, "Whatever you decide to do, remember that you can do whatever you want to do. Just put your mind to it, and don't let anyone or anything stop you from this day forward." I looked at Mr. Jones as my mentor. I can remember that day as if it was yesterday and those words have stuck with me throughout my life.

When I graduated from high school I moved to Detroit and then I later moved to Kansas City to run my Aunt's store. One day, I saw an Army commercial on television, "Be All You Can Be". I called the number and two days later I was on my way with a recruiter to take the Armed Services Vocational Aptitude Battery (ASVAB) test. I took the test and passed it, so I told my recruiter that I was ready to join, and I could leave that day. After talking with a military enlisted person, it was determined that the only job they had available that I could leave on that day was motor vehicle operator. They showed me that pay level, and it was a lot more money than I was making, and it came with benefits. I told him I would take it, my recruiter tried to talk me out of it and told me to wait for another job, but I told him if I didn't leave that day, I probably would not join. That was one of the best decisions that I made in my life. The recruiter took me home to pack my bag and took me back down to the Military Entrance Processing Center where I was sworn in and taken to the airport to fly to basic training. I called my mother and told her that I had joined the Army and that I would write her once I got an address.

After basic and my motor vehicle operator training, my first duty station was Fort Campbell, Kentucky. My pay was great, and I was able to send my Mom money each month to help with my siblings. After getting settled into my unit, I began working at the motor pool where the vehicles were kept. My squad leader was a white male Sergeant. The Sergeant's girlfriend came to the unit the same day that I got there; we later became friends. His girlfriend later became his wife. I didn't know it then, but as I looked back over my time in Sergeant White's squad, it becomes clear that he was prejudiced. He was always yelling at me and was verbally abusive. I know that I was not doing anything for him to treat me that way. I was someone who would and did follow orders. The effects of the Sergeant's negative treatment took its toll on me. It got so bad that one night when I was alone in my room, I thought about jumping out the third-floor window! I could not take the yelling from the Sergeant anymore. In that moment, I began to pray to the Lord, and He did not allow me to jump. I knew it was the power of God. I thank God for intervening that night and reminding me that there is nothing too hard for Him. I began to pray for the Sergeant and about two weeks later I injured my knee and was removed from his squad to do an office job. I knew it was God who answered my prayer.

After a year at Fort Campbell, Kentucky, I was on orders to Germany. I was now a Private First Class and moving overseas. The pay increase enabled me to send my Mom money to help with my siblings. It wasn't long before I was promoted to Specialist. Often, I would think about growing up in Mississippi; I never envisioned having money and being able to buy whatever I wanted. I wasn't the type of person to just spend money on anything, I was very frugal. However, I was appreciative to have sufficient money to take care of my needs and assist my family.

Shortly after my 22nd birthday, my mother passed; I was sent back to the States to attend the service. My younger brother, Wyndell, was also in the military and we had two younger sisters who had been home with our Mom. Our sisters went to stay with our Aunt and Uncle in Kansas City. Later that year, I re-enlisted and changed my job to become a chaplain assistant. While in school in New Jersey, a year after my mother's death, I got word that my brother had passed. I began to question God, "Why is this happening to me? God, where are you when it comes to my family?"

My first duty station, as a chaplain assistant, was with the Military District of Washington in Washington DC. It was a great assignment, and I loved my job. My First Sergeant authorized me to move off base in order to bring my sister, Marsha, to live with me. This afforded Marsha the opportunity for a better life and career. After getting another promotion to Staff Sergeant and about three years after Recruiting Duty, I was stationed at Fort Bragg, North Carolina. While at Fort Bragg, I deployed to Desert Shield Desert Storm, also known as the Gulf War. I had a great Chaplain but later found out that his faith was not in the Lord. We prayed with soldiers in our unit before the war began. After the war began my Chaplain began to look and act like he was afraid, and that we were going to die. He was not the same Chaplain that I knew. He stopped shaving and bathing. He had just gotten married before we left for the war and you could see it on his face; he was worried that he would not return to his wife. Soldiers in the unit began to ask what's wrong with him. We were in a medical brigade and I asked the female nurse if she would ask one of the psychologists to talk with him.

In the meantime, there was a white Master Sergeant (high ranking noncommissioned officer) in my unit who wanted me to report to him. In my job, I worked for the Chaplain, not the Master Sergeant. He was trying to make my job miserable. I began to pray for him that the hatred in his heart be removed. And I made it my business to speak to him every day. Finally, when the war was over the Chaplain was back to the person I knew. The Chaplain put me in for one of the highest awards and it was the white Master Sergeant who downgraded the award. The Chaplain was going to fight it, but I told him to leave it alone; I knew what award he wanted me to receive.

Once we returned from the war, I was assigned to a new Chaplain, and he was black. Our offices were in the chapel; it was the Chaplain and me. The soldiers who were in my Brigade worked out of their unit but would often come to the chapel. One day my boss, the Chaplain, came into my office and started massaging my shoulders and told me I was tense. I asked him to stop, and that I didn't appreciate him touching me. Sometime later, he took a military trip and asked me to pick him up from the airport when he returned. I assumed that I had to pick him up since it was a military trip. When he saw me, he gave me a hug, something I was not expecting, he was not my husband. I did let him know that I did not appreciate him hugging me. One day one of my male friends called the chapel and asked for me. My friend informed me that the Chaplain was questioning him; asking why he was calling and who was he. I told my friend that I had not received the message and I thanked him for telling me. Things got so bad I decided to go to my Chaplain's superior and inform him that the Chaplain was harassing me, and I had asked him on several occasions to stop. I told the Chaplain's superior that I just wanted to inform him and if I came back, I would like to press charges. I did not have any more problems with my Chaplain. I later got orders to go to Korea. Before I left the white Master Sergeant, who at one time seemed to have hated me, showed an attitude change. He was speaking and even having conversations with me. I said to myself, "Lord, I know it was you!" *If you have faith as small as a mustard seed, you can say to the mountains, 'Move from here to there' and it will move. Matthew 17:20*

After being in Korea for a few months, one of the soldiers from Fort Bragg sent me a letter telling me that the military was forcing the Chaplain who had harassed me to retire. There were allegations that he was dating one of the ladies he was counseling and that his wife was filing for divorce. God showed me that he will fight your battle. Leave it up to him. It reminds me of that song, *He May Not Come When You Want Him, but He's Right on Time.* I continued my military career, and I was faced with promotions passing me by; knowing that I had performed well above the standard and was deserving. I always had faith in the Lord and remembered where he had brought me from. I knew he would bring me through. I gave my promotions over to the Lord, and said- "Lord, you have BLESSED me with so much, and if you do not give me another promotion you have already done enough!" I also informed my praying sisters in Christ who were in agreement with me, and they offered up prayers on my behalf. When it was all said and done, the Lord promoted me to the highest rank in the Army that I could attain. God is good all the time and in every situation!

Being retired from the military and enjoying being a mentor to the young girls and boys I touch in the Atlanta Public Schools, year after year I share my story about my mentor and how he made a difference in my life and now I'm able to do the same. I enjoy going back to my hometown to participate in the programs for the senior citizens and youth that the organization plan for the year. "SHOW SOME LOVE" is my motto; ACTION speaks louder than words! As I look back over my life and see how the Lord has blessed me; I thank him for granting a little girl from a small town in Mississippi, growing up in the Projects, raised by a single mother of four... FAVOR.

I know my mother and brother are looking down upon me with a smile. Nobody but God; He has been so good to me. I truly believe that the favor of God came upon my life, when I was that little eight-year-old girl, crying in church and not fully understanding why. Yet, it was not until I began to have a relationship with Him that I really got to know Him. Now, I fully understand that He is someone you can go to, in the midnight hour. God is able no matter what you are going through. Just keep the faith. *"And we know that all things work together for good to those who love God, to those who are called according to His purpose."* Romans 8:28

I'm so thankful for my husband, daughter, sisters, family, and friends. To God be the Glory!

Nonprofit: www.connectingwinona.com

How Her Story Relates to My Story:

Author Roxie Blackmon

Roxie Blackmon

Roxie Blackmon was born in Durham, North Carolina, and has been residing in Accokeek, Maryland for the last nine years. She is an avid reader and absolutely loves arts and crafts. One of her most prized possessions is her music collection. Spanning the years, she has amassed hundreds of 78 & LP records and 45's to CD's and reel to reel tapes. Roxie grew up in East Orange, New Jersey and this is where she considers home.

Ms. Blackmon attended several colleges. She graduated from Western Pennsylvania School of Health and Business Technology and received her Associates and Bachelor of Science degrees in Computer Science and Information Systems Management from Park University.

Ms. Blackmon is also a twenty-five-year veteran of the United States Army. Master Sergeant Blackmon served in South Carolina, Texas, Georgia, Virginia, New Jersey, the Pentagon, Korea, and Kuwait. As an Information Systems Chief she deployed six times. Roxie currently works as a Developmental Test Lead for the Army's new automated personnel and pay system.

Sometimes You Have to Climb Over

Her story, my story is about the fears of a little black girl. I believe our stories start with our foundation. My foundation started in Roxboro, North Carolina on Sugar Hill. The city had an approximate population of 5500 residents in 1962. It is a lovely southern town, not particularly diverse, primarily inhabited by African American and Caucasian citizens, as were many small towns in the area. The main industries were built on slavery, with most of the residents still working in the tobacco and cotton fields. This is a town with lingering issues of light versus dark, rich versus poor, and some educated, and more with little or no education.

I often reflect on how your first memories can shape who you are, who you become, and maybe deep down, who you want to be. My first memories are those of isolation. People will say you can't possibly remember when you were nine months old, but I do. No, certainly not everything, but something that was profound for me. As I gazed around, the room I saw reds, yellow, and white flickering lights from the wood stove, felt the warmth on my skin, and I was dazzled by the beauty. I saw how the lights changed on my fingers and the bars of my crib. I saw my mommy and big sister across the room, in bed sleeping, so close, but so far away. I began to cry a little, to myself because I wanted to be over there, not trapped in my crib surrounded by bars. I scooted down to the edge of my mattress and tried reaching through to touch them, but I couldn't do it. Every night it seemed this was a recurring theme until a few weeks later, Fortunately, I mastered the art of climbing over the railing and joining them in their bed.

I remember when I was two years old, and my mom came home and said we're moving to New Jersey. I thought- "What's New Jersey? Is it down the street from Grandma's?" So, just like the Beverly Hillbillies, we loaded up the Chevy and moved to New Jersey and became a new family. We went from a family of three to living with a new stepfather, his mother and father, his sister, and her husband and their daughter. No, I didn't jump to another story. The first time I remember seeing my stepfather was when we were leaving North Carolina to travel to New Jersey. Hey, I was excited; now we had a family- like on television, which made us a loving family, right? Unfortunately, there were too many adults in one home, and that made life difficult. When your new family looked at your mother as the "poor, uneducated, black girl from the wrong side of town" it creates stress. While this may have been true, like all of us have experienced, it was not the whole story. So, once again we had to standup and dust ourselves off and climb over that hurdle and move on. A couple of years later we welcomed my little sister and the family dynamic changed. Now, I felt like that baby all over again, on the outside looking in. You, see my mother idolized my older sister and dad cherished his new baby, and I was just me. For me, it was best to stay quiet and not ask too many questions. You know the old adage- "children should be seen and not heard", that way you don't become the object of anger.

I have always loved to read, it's something special we did with my mom every Sunday evening before Wonderful World of Disney came on. I would read everything, cereal boxes, labels, junk mail, newspapers, anything. My grandparents could not read or write, so my mother would write letters for my aunts to read to them. She had written a letter for my grandmother and left it on the nightstand, and of course, I read it. It said, "That girl is a liar just like her dad", I dropped it like it was on fire and went to my room. I shouldn't have read it, but she raised me to be curious, just not *that* curious. Unfortunately, this only re-enforced my anxiety and self-doubt in myself and it would take years for me to climb out from under that hole. This minor event setup my defining role within the family, seen but not heard, the quiet one. By the time I was nine, I was becoming a young lady and began dealing with the complications that brought on. Life-changing distrust followed, no longer a child, but not quite a woman, what a mountain to climb.

I started high school at thirteen. I was so excited: new school, new experiences, and new friends. After a month, I spied a flyer to try out for the cheerleading squad. "That's it; that's what I want to do!" I had been on an intramural city drill team for the last three years; it should be a lock. The only hitch was that you must have a physical before tryouts even started. So, my mom made an appointment with our general practitioner, and Dad took me over there after work. Everything was going fine until the doctor asked my dad to step out and asked me how long I had been having sex? I said, "I'm not having sex." The doctor had my dad come back in and he said to my dad, "It looks like your daughter is pregnant. You know how these young girls are. Sometimes, they just don't want to tell you."

To say everything turned to crap, from that point, is an understatement. We went home, and I had to hear how I was the *lowest of the low* from him. However, it was even worst when my mother came home and without listening or believing my rebuttals, she immediately began condemning me, too. A couple of days later, she made an appointment for me to see her gynecologist. I was terrified to have some strange man touching me. I couldn't believe all this happened simply because I wanted to be a cheerleader. Being naïve I began thinking that maybe I had done something without knowing, or maybe I shouldn't have sat on that toilet seat, crazy right? Hey, this was 1976, no rapid tests, the only thing he could tell my mother was that my hymen was intact. He went on to say- "Doesn't mean she's not pregnant, some boys' penises are small when they are young". Now, we had to make more appointments, more distrust, and more mental anguish. When all the testing, x-rays, CT scans were done, it turned out I was born with an ovarian cyst that began growing when I started my menstrual cycle at nine years old. So, after the removal of my left ovary, a week in the hospital, and eight weeks of recovery, I still didn't get an apology from the people I loved and trusted the most. So, needless to say, this became another hill to climb. I did finally get back to school, I missed the opportunity to be a cheerleader and I missed experiencing the wonders of your first four months of high school and the bonds you forge.

My home life never really stabilized after that, there was always distrust and apprehension. My feeling of being on outside now included not being accepted. I dreamed of graduation and moving into a new life. However, I could not move quite that fast. Somethings still lingered from the past. Somethings changed and somethings did not last. I guess that was another thing to climb over.

Why are these foundation stories important? Why does it make a difference forty years later? As I stated earlier, the foundation stories are your core. The more you fight against yourself and understanding your foundation stories, the more confusing things may seem. The confusion could become one more thing that you have to climb over.

What I have found is the experiences of childhood led to dysfunctional relationships and personal sabotage. For example, I got married after swearing, that once I left home, I would never allow anyone to have that much control over me ever again! But I so desperately wanted to believe someone would unconditionally love me for who I was. So, I ignored my inner warnings and placed my love and trust in the wrong person.

I was a young soldier, in the Army Reserve, about to leave active duty, and because my specialty job had taken thirty-eight weeks to complete the training, with a ten percent attrition rate, the Army offered me a wavier to switch over to active duty without having to wait the required six months. The first mistake, I consulted my then-boyfriend about what I should do, and he said, "Don't do that, just come down here to Georgia with me". Second mistake, not taking that opportunity to see if I could excel. These decisions resulted in more life-learning lessons to climb over. I found myself dependent on another's emotional instability, financial and professional judgement, and my own naiveté. I awoke from the euphoria of the moment, once again isolated and reliant, trying to figure out how to escape a bad marriage. Over the next six years, I seemed to go from one emergency to another, one life- changing obstacle to the next. What I learned is, I am my greatest resource. Through ectopic pregnancies, to infidelity, outside children, to actually fighting for a divorce, it became abundantly clear- the fall is ooh so easy but climb takes time.

I am sure as you are reading, you are saying- "How do all of these things correlate?" Think about it in another light. Think about that two-year-old just wanting to be near her loved ones. I think about how my home life which was built on a foundation grounded in industries that were built on slavery, working in the tobacco and cotton fields, where it's light vs dark, rich vs poor, and my family was a combination of educated, and a few uneducated. The struggle to climb was not just our skin color or geographic location; it was our mindset and level of determination. Some people reading will feel sorry for that little girl or have anger towards the adults in her life. However, that's not my intent. My intent is to show that everyone is made from the synthesis of their experiences: good or bad and this includes the people who become a part of their life.

For example, my love of art was fostered by my kindergarten art teacher, Ms. Glover. A striking young African American teacher, tall and light brown-skinned. She was always impeccably dressed, always nice to the students, and ready to assist and help everyone make the craftiest doodad to take home. Ms. Glover took us from Paper Mache' Christmas balls to rope rugs and baskets. She was able to make you feel as if you had created the most wonderful thing in the world. When I was in 5th grade and again in junior high school, she became my Vice Principal at both schools. She was still the same beautiful lady, trying to inspire young African American children to reach for the sky. I was able to take her encouraging words to heart when dreaming of what I might become. To be reminded you are doing a good job, that what you are creating or participating in are integral parts of the school community and have lasting results, had an impact. I began to see how my community in East Orange New Jersey was reforming my ideals and how I looked at the opportunities and resources that were available to me.

By the time I was prepared to graduate, we had a population of roughly 75,000 residents, and 85 percent of them were Black or African American, and we had our city's first Black Mayor. In 1980, East Orange High School, had approximately 3500 students with around 650 graduating, and of that number 70 percent went on to attend college or technical schools. We were the children of the Civil Rights Movement's changes and strides; we were by a large amount the first generation of high school graduates for most families. This generation was able to see beyond stereotypical expectations of menial workers, the barrier of low aspirations, and even lower incomes. We were able to climb beyond the trappings of the inner city, beyond the bad advice from guidance counselors, beyond the fear to leave the comfort and familiarity of home in order to experience the unknown. We were inspired to climb even if we fell: to dust ourselves off and try again. This ability to look for challenges and find solutions gave me the fortitude to move on, but not forget my foundations.

Years later, as I look back at the friends, colleagues, and soldiers I had the pleasure of working with and often guiding or being guided by, I am grateful. Over those years, I often had life-altering decisions to make, and by talking and/or counseling, I made it through. I think that the fear of failure and use of selective blindness only made my problems larger. I too have been prone to procrastination and worry, and at those points, I found myself still fearful of the unknown future of my actions. Still unsure of how I fit in, or how I would be viewed by my family and friends. In some ways, I will always be the same person inside as I have always been, but in other ways, I can step out and look back at everything with adult eyes.

I can only reflect on the facts; I was born to parents that split before even seeing me. Raised by parents that didn't *see* me, married a man who didn't really love me, and was hampered by preconceived notions of who I should be. It has been challenging to restart over and over, and sometimes over again. Once when I left home, once when I initially went to college, and when that did not work, once when I joined the military, once again in divorce, once again going through bankruptcy and health problems, and lastly when finding the ability to try to love again. As a rule, you cannot let situations bind you, or keep you stagnate in your actions or decisions. Even if you were born on the backs of slavery, with most of your family still working in the tobacco and cotton fields, and all around you they are still trying to base your worth on whether you are light or dark-skinned, rich or poor, educated or uneducated, you still can accomplish many things. I am a mixture of all the heartache, all the hopes and dreams, and all the unasked and unanswered questions of the past. Each climb starts the same way, one step at a time. Now, it's clear to me, my mother placed me on the other side of the room to be closer to the woodstove so I could stay warm. As I grew older, she did not focus on me so much because she thought I was self-sufficient. I wonder if I had known these truths if my family dynamics would have been different. Would it have affected the way I view everything? Would my life have been different, or would it still have turned out the same?

My partner asked if I was sure, I wanted all these things published. I said, "Yes, somewhere out there is another little girl or boy who wants to climb high or climb out or climb over a railing. It is worth the risk of transparency if by sharing my stories, I can show them that with perseverance and a little elbow grease, the stains do come out in the wash!

How Her Story Relates to My Story:

_____

_____

_____

_____

_____

_____

_____

_____

_____

_____

_____

Author Ruby "WooWoo" Murray

Ruby "WooWoo" Murray

Education breeds confidence. Confidence breeds hope. Hope breeds peace.
~Confucius.

The opportunity to provide a sense of confidence, hope, and peace
for students influenced Ruby Murray's desire to become a high
school JROTC teacher. Her decision to enter the field of education
was a direct result of 26-years of service in the United States Army
where she coached, educated, and positively impacted thousands of
soldiers and Department of the Army (DA) civilians. While serving
in the military, Ruby was fortunate to demonstrate to soldiers that
success is within everyone's grasp. Now, she is grateful to provide
her students with the same life lesson.

Most influential to Ruby's ability to relate well to students was
her supportive father who believed in her, even during the times
when she had trouble believing in herself. He instilled in her the
importance of moral integrity and a high work ethic. With a desire
to honor my father's influence, Ruby continues to dedicate her life to
not only changing the lives of others but providing the support,
strength, and encouragement that her students may not otherwise
receive. Ruby strongly believes that the best way to transform
someone's life is through education, and that begins with effective
teaching and solid leadership. For Ruby, it is one task to simply teach
children, but to know that she has helped to positively mold their
lives for the better is far more significant. Her greatest
accomplishment in education is preparing her students to be
successful in the field of their choosing. Each student who
tells Ruby that she has changed and inspired their lives for the better,
makes her feel as though she has completed yet another
mission. Her various interactions with people over the years
have convinced her that educating our children is essential to our
future and improving our way of life. Because her first teacher,
her father, served as her biggest supporter and instilled in her that
she could be anything she put her mind to, she is now living

out her predestined calling! Daily, she aspires to teach children the necessary academic skills and life lessons that her father taught her.

Ruby always looks to Heaven and smiles at her dad, knowing that she made the choice to be an educator after serving in the military and that she appreciated him for instilling in her the courage and mindset that she could be anything that she wanted to be in this life. The message from her father, is the same one that she conveys to the kids that she teaches, reminding them that they are all destined for greatness. Because of her dad's constant positive reinforcement, she understands the necessity of going beyond teaching academics. Living out her destiny, she teaches life lessons that bring her students confidence, hope, and peace.

Ruby Murray is the wife of Alfred Murray and the mother of Jasmine Murray.

Finding the "How" to the "Why"

My "WHY" was My Daughter. I was searching to discover my "How".

When I was young, I was always willing to do just about anything for the knowledge and experience. I was the type of kid who dreamed big but never understood how to achieve those dreams. I always wanted a better life for myself but didn't know how to get there. I was an average student, but I played almost every sport from basketball to track, and I was even a cheerleader for the wrestling team. Growing up on the Eastern Shore of Virginia, we only had three options for work. These options were employment at either Perdue or Holly Farms chicken plants or on a local farm as a tomato grader. I was not a big fan of live chickens, so I settled for the position of tomato grader at the local farm during the summer to pay for school clothes. Through my mother, I learned the value of hard work early on. My mother instilled divine independence in me.

One day while watching television, a commercial came on with a man in a white hat with a star in the middle. This man was pointing his finger saying: "I WANT YOU FOR THE U.S. ARMY". At that moment, something inside me clicked, and I felt a surge of energy from within. I was sure this was my calling from God for a new beginning. This commercial also triggered strong memories of both my father and grandfather because they were both proud, hardworking, and humble men. They both said to me on several occasions prior to their deaths, "You better make something out of yourself. Get off the Eastern Shore and never look back." I will be forever grateful for their advice because I took their words to heart and never looked back.

I joined the United States Army in 1989, directly after high school. This was my first time ever leaving Virginia, and it was an emotional roller coaster. I was afraid of where I was headed and where it might lead, but the voices of my father and grandfather constantly echoed in the back of my mind, telling me to make something of myself. As a black woman, I already knew and was constantly reminded by the world that I had three prominent factors working against me. One, I was black, two, I was a female, and three, I was a black female entering what was thought of as a man's profession. This did not slow me down because I was determined to prove the world wrong and claim my seat at the table.

My military journey started in Fort Jackson, South Carolina, where I attended basic training. From there, I went to Fort Lee, Virginia, for advanced training and watched my career take off like a rocket going into space. While I served in the military my life was great. I was a passionate leader on a mission and the type of leader who enjoyed giving back to my community. "Was" is the keyword. My life hit a brick wall. I was in pain, but I did not know where the pain was coming from. I was sick and constantly throwing up, with terrible headaches. I remember going into my bedroom and asking my husband to take me to the emergency room because I was not feeling good. Upon my arrival at the emergency room, they checked all my vital signs and asked for me to urinate in a cup and drew my blood. I waited for hours for them to call me to the back to be seen by a doctor. Finally, I was called, and the doctor started smiling as he informed me, I was pregnant.

I cried happy tears with the knowledge that I was becoming a mother. As the months went by, I started showing my little baby bump. I knew I was eating more and gaining weight as I tried my hardest to remain physically fit because I was a soldier. After giving birth to my beautiful daughter, Jasmine, my weight took a turn for the worst. I went from wearing a size 8 to 10 to buying a size 16 to 18 in pants. The military had strict guidelines, and I was in jeopardy of getting kicked out. I knew in my mind that I did not want to go back home, but most importantly, I did not want to disappoint my grandfather and father. I realized my body would never be the same as before. To top it off, I gained nearly 90 pounds post-pregnancy. I was unable to put on my pants; my shirts were extremely tight, and when I looked at myself in the mirror, tears would stream down my face. Depression and Post Traumatic Stress Disorder were slowly starting to take over my life. I felt like I was in a small box and couldn't find a way out because everything was so dark.

One day, I started flipping through the yellow pages looking for a personal trainer - someone who could help me find my "Happy Place" all over again. I found myself at an all-women's Fitness Gym with a great trainer. But after about 2 weeks, the urge to give up was overwhelming. My legs would not stop rubbing together, and I would just cry. So, one day I entered the gym and told my trainer it would be my last day because it was too hard for me. My postpartum depression and the negative comments from the outside world had gotten under my skin. In my mind, I was done. I could not do it anymore. I remember my trainer telling me to give it another shot, but this time she started talking to me about what motivates me. As a small tear fell from my eyes, I told her my beautiful daughter Jasmine was my motivation. She instructed me to bring a picture of my daughter the next time I came in and to give it one more chance to work before throwing in the towel. So, the next day I did exactly what she asked me to do. I brought in a picture of my daughter and looked at it each time I wanted to give up. All I could see were her big brown eyes looking at me, and from that point on, I used my daughter's photo as my motivation. After I completed my one-hour workout session, I remember my trainer coming over to me and asking how I felt now. I remember saying, all I needed was her all along to give me the willpower and strength to never give up! My daughter's picture became my heartbeat each day I got up to get ready for the gym. She became my "WHY" on "HOW" I could not and would not give up!

I had a major turning point in my life; it was like no other energy or feeling I had felt before. I started working out seven days a week instead of six days. As the months went by, I started seeing a transformation take over my body in a positive way. I had joy from within, knowing I did not have the feeling of my legs rubbing together when I got on the treadmill. My old clothes started to fit again, and all I could do was smile and thank God for not letting go of me. He gave me the perseverance I needed to push that rock out of my way in order to make it to my finish line.

I realized I was a week out from finishing maternity leave and going back to work after giving birth to my daughter. I had to prepare myself to get weighed-in and taped, in order to avoid getting put out of the military. My brain literally went into anxiety and depression because I did not know what my future would hold. I remember signing back into my unit on a Monday morning, and my leadership letting me know I would be having a Physical Fitness Test, weigh in and tape test sometime that month. I replied with "Hooah, Sergeant." My mind was all over the place waiting for the day to come because I feared the outcome. Yet I still had the confidence and the motivation from within that I was going to pass everything. When that morning finally came for me to take my Physical Fitness Test, which consisted of push-ups, sit-ups, and the two-mile run, I passed it with flying colors! I had one more hurdle to jump, and that was getting weighed in and taped. They measured my hips, neck, wrist and waist areas. After they took the measures three times in each area, they told me to step out and wait in the hallway. I waited anxiously with nervous sweat running down my back and sweat beading on my forehead. Finally, the wait was over, and the sergeant called me back in and told me I passed my Physical Training and Tape Test, and that I did not have to take another test until 6 months later. Walking out of the building, I cried all the way to my car. Once in my car, I turned on some gospel music and looked at my motivation, which was my daughter's picture. Then I cried even more. I made it, and she was the reason "WHY" and she was my "HOW".

By fulfilling my goals and aspirations, I felt God was not through with me yet! From that point forward, my motivation was on a natural high, and I was refusing to give up! I even started working out twice a day, and it felt really good. One day, while I was working out during a high-intensity Cardio Training, I remember someone yelling, "Hey, High-Speed, when you get done, please come and see me!" It was our battalion Command Sergeant Major. After my workout session was over, I proceeded to his office and waited for his secretary to let him know I was there. His secretary directed me back down the hall to his office on the right. Once I got into his office, I remember him telling me he was impressed with me working out every day. He explained that he and other leadership often had professional conversations about how I could help with a new pilot program that was coming to Fort Bragg, which was the Postpartum/Anti-partum Physical Fitness program. They were looking for instructors, and I was a perfect fit! He informed me that he would be reaching out to my leadership to let them know that I would be one of the instructors who would be reporting every morning to assist with this new pilot program, which was a 6-month tasking. He asked me if I was up for the challenge to tackle this mission. I smiled and said, "Yes, Command Sergeant Major!"

It was a cold morning on the first day that I reported for my train-the-trainer classes with some other instructors. The classes were very intense because they were teaching us everything we were supposed to do as instructors when it came to dealing with females who were in the Postpartum Physical Training program. These were the women who were ready to get back into shape, based on their doctors' orders on what they could and could not do. On my first day as a postpartum instructor, I remember having over 50 females from all walks of life and shapes and sizes. My job was to motivate them through personal experience and recently acquired techniques to get back into the best shape possible. I needed them to not only trust me, but to also trust the process. I knew all too well how they might be feeling. I shared my story and then explained that for some, this journey would be full of uphill battles. I went on to state, that with every battle that came their way, I was going to help them find their "Happy Place" once again. The program required the participants to still report to their units after each session and perform all their normal duties. Many thought they would not be able to complete the course and perform their normal duties at the same time. It was then that I applied a special ingredient called - LOVE for one another. Each female had their own story to tell, but they all knew their "WHY"; they did not want to be chaptered out of the military. I, along with the other instructor, provided the "HOW" through mentorship so they could throw away the word FAILURE and turn it into a positive word called FAITH, for the sake of the sons or daughters they brought in this world.

Over the years, the Postpartum and Anti-Partum Program grew, and I became the Senior Exercise Leader for the entire Fort Bragg base. I was a game-changer and all local news media, newspapers, and Army Times always felt they could get a good news story from the amazing program on Fort Bragg. The program was so successful that other military installations used Fort Bragg as a model for the rest of the United States Army bases. My dedication and commitment to the Fort Bragg Postpartum Physical Fitness Program was successful. I was able to get over 300 females back to their preferred body weight throughout the nine years I was able to be an instructor. I inspired women and allowed them to take back a positive mindset, their best bodies ever and spiritual souls to "find their happy place once again, and even better".

Because of my own trials and tribulations, I was the type of leader who pushed soldiers up, not out. I used my life experiences to help other women see the light at the end of their tunnel. I like to think of myself as an agent of change, contributing to the transformation of the lives of many women. I consider it an honor to be trusted by each one of them, as they allowed me to help them through their most difficult times. Still today, I am able to impact so many women and even men, by showcasing my talent and changing lives, one person at a time.

I was able to weather the storm early in my career, it allowed me to be a testament to show others that their testimony is anointed as well! It showed them to never give up hope and to always believe that if they could envision something as amazing as carrying a baby for nine long months, then they could certainly achieve their goals of reshaping their bodies and their lives. As I look back on my life's journey and reflect on the words of my father and grandfather, I am not sure I fully understood what they meant when they told me to make something of myself. But today, I understand the impact I've had on other peoples' lives has allowed me to far exceed my expectations. I've made far more of myself than I could have ever dreamed possible.

Her Story Relates to My Story:

_____

_____

_____

_____

_____

_____

_____

_____

_____

_____

_____

_____

Author Dr. Shelly L Walker

Dr. Shelly L Walker

Dr. Shelly L. Walker is a native of Pittsburgh, Pennsylvania, and is the youngest of a blended family of five boys and five girls. She is married with two sons. She was educated in the public schools of Pittsburgh, Pennsylvania, has a Bachelor's in Psychology, Minors in Political Science and Sociology from Troy State University, a Master's in Psychology with an emphasis in Marriage Family Therapy from Chapman University, and a Doctorate in Educational Psychology from Capella University. Her published thesis is entitled: *The Lived Experiences of Teachers as They Describe Their Values and Ethics Within the Educational School System.*

She is an active member of several community organizations, that includes the Order of the Eastern Stars, Daughters: an auxiliary of the Ancient Egyptian Arabic Order Nobles Mystic Shrine, Order of the Golden Circle, and Delta Sigma Theta Sorority, Inc.

Before getting married and following her husband's military service career, Dr. Walker began her professional career as a Sexual Assaults Counselor in Pittsburgh, helping girls who had been physically and/or sexually abused. She also worked as an Instructional Aid for the School for the Blind.

Currently, Dr. Walker serves as a Transition Program Analyst. She is also the CEO of *Theories of Life Counseling Services and serves* as a Marriage Family Therapist. Dr. Walker provides counseling services, mentorship, and motivational speaking for all ages, and advocates for Domestic Violence at Fear2Freedom Alliance.

Dr. Walker can be reached by email:
walkernwalkerccs@theoriesoflife.org or at www.walkernwalkerccs.com

The "Dues" and "Don'ts" of Discrimination

April 2015 - Wow! I did not know her, and she did not know me. But somehow, my new first-line supervisor believed that she knew everything about me. She illegally presumed that she had heard everything she needed to know about me and was therefore, able to judge me. Never would anyone ever think that the misuse of the word "Do" instead of the word "Due," would lead to two years of manipulation, hate, and a lengthy discrimination case. Out of jealousy, my supervisor's demand for superiority created a toxic working environment. There was continuous belittlement and anguish over the misuse of a word in an email. Fast forward.

August 2015- An Email. "Do to scheduling conflicts, the session for Thursday will need to be rescheduled" was met with the response from my first-line supervisor, "Thank you for sending the email. Not sure if the staff was included in the email. Please forward it to them in case we have walk-ins. On another note, please ensure correct spelling when forwarding emails out. Though, I do understand we all make mistakes." My response to her, "Will do! Sorry about the spelling. Not sure if you are aware that I am Dyslexic. Normally I try to review my writing, but I was in a rush leaving out. Today is my husband's birthday". Fast forward.

November 2015- Appraisal Time. I received a low-performance rating from my second-line supervisor. Of course, I questioned the rating. My second-line supervisor listed on my appraisal that I "listen and communicate well but needs to work on written communication to get to the next level. Is a good worker but paying attention to detail is needed to progress to the next level". I asked her where the feedback was coming from. She stated that my rating was input from my first-line supervisor. I was shocked. I had never received a low-performance rating before. I had been at my job for eight years and did not understand the justification of my appraisal. I further questioned the rating and asked for an example or incident. Low and behold, the "dues" email from April was being negatively held against me. I told my second-line supervisor, along with all the staff, aware that I was dyslexic. I explained that when the email incident had occurred in April, I had informed my first-line supervisor that I was dyslexic. Although dyslexic is a learning disability, it has not prevented me from accomplishing my work and indeed has not stopped me from obtaining a Doctoral degree.

Before leaving the room, I informed my second-line supervisor that I disagreed with their justification for a low-performance rating, and their insensitivity to my disability. I don't know if they did not believe me or if I intimated them. Despite the circumstances, their attitudes and actions lead all involved down a rabbit hole of a check and checkmate. Their open denial and emboldened demeanor were inexcusable. Fast forward.

February 2016- Denied Promotion. For months, my first-and-second-line supervisors unfairly continued to deny me a promotion. Although I was an internal employee and made it to the phone interview, I was not selected. An external employee from a different center was selected. When I asked why I was not selected, my second-line supervisor stated that it was my writing. I then asked my second-line supervisor if she remembered that I had informed her of my disability and believed that she was using my writing disability to discriminate against me and hold me from promotions. The most discriminating issue is that the promotion was for a position and grade that I previously had and had performed exceptionally well. I was no longer in the position because I wanted to be secure in a permanent position, complete school, and not have to commute so far from home. I volunteered to the lower position on the condition of retaining my pay. How was it, according to my first, second, and somehow my third-line supervisors, I was not promotable to a position that I previously held. Fast forward.

April 2016- Unprofessional Conduct. By this time, any other person may have gone postal. I kept my poise during their cat-and-mouse games, even when my second-line supervisor became resentful and irrational. During a training session, she blew off the handle. She thought I passed a note and was talking about her to a co-worker. She screamed, "Stop being childish" and stormed out of the training. My first line supervisor jumped up and stated, "If the shoes fit, then wear it" and she left the training as well. My co-workers and I looked at each other in disbelief. It was not until I explained to them what occurred that they realized the supervisors were the ones who behaved unprofessionally. After that incident, my supervisors avoided having any direct interaction with me. Perhaps, this was a result of their feeling of being paranoid and guilty. Fast forward.

May 2016- Discrimination Complaint. I had enough and filed an Equal Employment Opportunity (EEO) Office complaint. After filing my complaint, I was informed of my rights, informed of the option of Alternate Dispute Resolution (ADR), and my responsibility to present any evidence for my case. During the process of collecting the evidence for my complaint, I was informed that the person selected for the position declined the position. Right there, one would think the discrimination case closed and that they would place me in the position. Hopefully, no one held their breath. My supervisors selected another external person, less qualified, and I was the one who had to train her for the duties that she would be performing.

Shortly afterward, they asked me if I was interested in Alternative Dispute Resolution (ADR), and if so, my Squadron Commander preferred that I mediate with my third-line supervisor instead of him. I questioned if my third-line supervisor would have the authority to address my remedies during mediation. I was told that my third-line supervisor had the authority to a certain extent. That the Commander and Civilian Personnel Office (CPO) would be on standby if needed. I went ahead and agreed to ADR with my third-line supervisor. Fast forward.

July 2016- Mediation. The mediator reviewed the process and explained his role and informed my third-line supervisor that she and I could speak freely. I told my third-line supervisor what my second-line supervisor stated about my performance rating. I explained that the comments she said about me were why I knew they were discriminating against me. My third-line supervisor felt that there were discrimination incidents. She stated that I had the second-highest score for the position. I asked her to provide the scoring sheets. She stated that the scoring sheets were destroyed. I questioned why they destroyed the scoring sheets and why I was not placed in the position once the person selected declined the position. The mediator asked what remedies I was seeking. I told him that I wanted to be placed in the higher-grade position and for my first-line supervisor to receive supervisory training.

My third-line supervisor stated that she believed she could not place me in the competitive position I applied for, but I could apply again. I told her that it did not make sense to apply for a position I was discriminated against and that this was my second time applying for a position that I previously held. She then replied that she might be able to place me in a non-competitive position. I questioned if that was possible. The mediator consulted with other EEO staff. The EEO staff consulted with CPO. I asked the mediator to check with CPO a second time before signing the agreement. The Settlement Agreement was for me to be placed in a non-competitive position by 1 October 2016. Once again, one would think the case would have been closed. That was far from the end. Fast forward.

August 2016- The Switch-up. My third-line supervisor told me that the CPO informed her that I could not be placed in the non-competitive position until a Request for Personnel Action (RPA) at the end of the fiscal year, September 31, 2016. In the meantime, my second-and third-line supervisors asked me to consider the duties of a different position and moving me out of my office to a shared office with another employee. They explained that the other employee and I would have similar duties and could collaborate. I had no objections to the suggested position and sharing an office with the proposed employee. I stated, "yes", but with the condition that they meet my required accommodation. The lighting would need to be modified because I suffered from migraines. For eight years, I had my own office, which allowed me to control the lighting without affecting other employees. Subsequently, I received an email from the Union asking if I agreed with sharing an office and if my accommodations were complied with. The short answer was "no". Fast forward.

September 2016- Not Surprised. I went to my third-line supervisor to see if she heard from the CPO. I had not seen or received any notification of the promotion nor the suggested position. My third-line supervisor stated that she submitted the paperwork and asked me to provide copies of my employee records. My third-line supervisor came to me a day or so later. She stated that CPO informed her that I did not meet the qualifications of the position. I needed to provide copies of my employee records showing that I had held the higher-grade position. I did not understand this new justification, but I provided her my employee records. Weeks went by. In mid-October, my third-line supervisor told me that she did not have the authority to place me in either position or I would not receive the promotion. Here we go again. Continued discrimination, a manipulated false reasoning, and the brazen breach of the Settlement Agreement. Fast forward.

December 2016- Into the Fire. Even though they had not promoted me or placed me in either position, my first-and third-line supervisors proceeded to move me out of my office. I was forced to file a formal complaint about the Settlement Agreement breach and now a union complaint about the change in working condition with no provided accommodations. There were weeks of discussions between the EEO and the Union office. They had a staff member search the storage area and other work sections for light bulbs. They had her standing on desks measuring lighting fixtures, all while my assigned union representative concealed her bias of me. The union representative and my third-line supervisor were friends. She did not provide me with proper representation, and she had no intention of resolving my case. Instead, she merely went through the motions: pretending to represent me.

Dealing with the two employee-related cases and $8,000 in lawyer fees, it all became overwhelming for me. While sitting at the front desk, a sharp pain started in my chest. Thinking it was a gas bubble, I went to my office to relax and see if it would go away. The pain sharpened and my heartbeat became more rapid. I stood up, but my legs buckled. I fell. I grabbed ahold of my desk. My door was closed, and I began to panic. I crawled to the phone and called the front desk. My co-workers came running. I was curled up on the floor. My co-workers tried to lift me from the floor into a chair, but I did not want to sit in a chair. The chest pain increased. Somehow, I ended up in the hallway. The pain intensified. The medics arrived. They ran an EKG while I was on the floor. Then they tried laying me on the gurney to get a proper EKG reading. I started fighting them. I felt that I would have stopped breathing if I laid on my back. Fear was on my co-worker's faces. One co-worker started crying. I started crying. I heard someone said to call her husband.

I was transported to Urgent Care, curled up on my side and holding my chest. Hours of blood work, x-rays, and EKGs were done. All tests and scans were good; the doctors had no explanation for my pain. The **doctor's diagnosis** was that I had experienced a panic attack. However, he cautiously referred me to a Cardiologist and Pulmonologist. All went well with the Cardiologist, but not with the Pulmonologist. The Pulmonologist diagnosed me with asthma from environmental factors and emotional stress. Fast forward.

February 2017- The Move. The union representative that was representing me took another job. She left no notes. I had to start all over with a new union representative. Eventually, they moved me, but not into a shared office. I was forced into a shared cubicle with three other employees and only provided accommodation with two tabletop lamps to adjust the lighting. I did not allow the move to break my spirits. The move strengthened my relationships with my co-workers. My co-workers became readily comfortable relying on me so much that I applied for the lead consultant position. Once again, I was not selected but had to train the person chosen for the position. I remained professional. I added their retaliations and incidents to the discrimination case. Fast forward

June 2017- New Supervisor. My first-line supervisor is now my second-line supervisor, and the new employee became my first-line supervisor. Most would think that my now second-and third-line supervisors' discriminating behaviors would have come to an end. Their discontent that the staff respected me more than them, lead them to try to upstage me every chance they could. I remained professional. The reassurance from my family and co-workers convinced me to end my second and third-line supervisors' harassment. I applied for a position outside the agency and was selected. Fast forward

June 2018- Happy. I relied on faith. I was successful and performed so well in the new position that I placed my EEO complaint in the Lord's hands. I withdrew my complaint and shortly after was selected for an even higher position with more responsibility. Fast forward.

August 2018- Satisfaction. You would not believe it. Low and behold, I ended up having to work with my once first-line supervisor: the one who was promoted and became my second-line supervisor. She had told me that I would never achieve. Yet, I was in a higher position! There was dissatisfaction on her face when she saw me sitting in the chair next to her. No one in the room knew what had occurred between the two of us, but her guilt made her pick up her belongings and move to a chair behind me. I provided her my best victory smile and turned in the chair, leaving my back to her. God is good all the time!

How Her Story Relates to My Story:

_____

_____

_____

_____

_____

_____

_____

_____

_____

_____

_____

_____

Author Terri Moten-Jackson

Terri Moten-Jackson

Terri Moten-Jackson is a proud native of Gary, Indiana. She is the mother of five beautiful children and the grandmother of one beautiful granddaughter, Giovanna. She gave her life to Christ at the age of 16 years old at Trinity Missionary Baptist Church in Gary, Indiana. She graduated in 1988 from West Side High School. She moved to New Jersey in 1999 when her stars aligned with her partner David and currently resides in Atco, New Jersey. She graduated in 2012 with her Associates Degree in Paralegal Studies. She is incredibly involved in the Eastern Stars and has served as the Worthy Matron of her Chapter three times and served as District Deputy Grand Matron for Oziel Grand Chapter.

Currently, Terri is serving as 1st Lieutenant Commandress for Zamora Court No. 135. Terri is currently employed with AmerisourceBergen where she has been for the past six years in the Accounts Payable Department. She has always had that entrepreneurial spirit and in 2020 she began her career as a Paparazzi Independent Consultant. Her family and her true friends bring her life, and she has been blessed to have devoted friends that have helped her along her journey.

Unwritten

Where does one begin to tell the story of abuse? It is hard to put into words, as it is unlike anything you have ever experienced. When I was 20 years old, I met my ex-husband during a time when I felt abandoned and lonely. My mother had just put me out of her house. She did this because I was very rebellious. My ex-husband quickly stepped in like a knight in shining armor to "rescue" me. The first two months were our honeymoon season, and everything was great. Then came the argument over something trivial and the first push came as a surprise, along with an apology that it would never happen again; I believed him. Then came the second, third, and other physical encounters; it was becoming routine. I left my ex-husband, but for only three weeks. He continued to call and beg me to come back. If I knew then what I know now, I would have never answered any of his calls. I went back to more promises that it would never happen again. The promise of love, filled in for the lack of self-love that I was experiencing. I was broken. Although the abuse got worse, I stayed. I felt alone; I had nowhere to go. I had no money and had a job that barely paid me to live on my own. I became pregnant. I was beaten for being pregnant and forced to have an abortion. I got the message that I needed to take care of it as soon as possible. I did as I was told. My ex-husband did not go with me to provide the support that I needed; my girlfriend went instead. After all that I endured, I still stayed with him. Three months later, I was pregnant again and was forced to have another abortion. Months later, I gave up my apartment and moved in with him and his mom, thinking that would help, but it did not. Once again, I was pregnant, but this time I decided to keep the baby. Pregnancy did not stop the abuse. It made it worse. I cried every single day and was abused even more. I was pushed, shoved, slapped, and punched. He was careful that the bruises I had, no one could see.

He took me out one night with friends and the entire night he talked about how bad I looked and how the other women looked so much better than me. As if I didn't already have enough to deal with, alcohol began to consume him. He started cheating on me, and I would find condoms under his car's floor mats. He would stay out all night long and leave me home with his mother. The more I begged and pleaded for him to stay home, the more he went out. I stayed with this man because I felt that I had nowhere to go and no one to turn to.

After my daughter was born, we began to look for a house. We bought our first house when she was seven months old. Soon after that, he proposed, and I was so happy because I thought the natural progression was to get married. I was so warped that in my mind; I did not want to be the reason he had to spend extra money, so I agreed to get married at the Justice of the Peace. I robbed myself of that fairytale experience because that is what he wanted. The day after we got married, he beat me for spending $20.00. The abuse went on and on; the beatings got worse. I was trapped, a young mother with a baby with nowhere to go. I started making friends and had a good girlfriend that worked with me. Sometimes she would come over and spend the weekend with me, but she never knew that my husband beat me. The day came when she finally learned my secret. She was at my house and, he called me upstairs. I had taken a different job that paid me12 cents an hour less but was closer to home. While my best friend was there, I was upstairs with my husband, being beaten for two hours. My girlfriend feared him and was scared for me. When she left, she never came back. Again, I was alone and exactly where he wanted me to be, alienated from everyone.

In addition to the alcohol, he began to abuse drugs, and his drug of choice was crack cocaine. In between the fights, we maintained a sexual relationship, and I became pregnant with my son. I was praying that this pregnancy would cause him to stop the abuse. I hoped that it would give him the motivation to show his son how he was supposed to be as a man; it didn't. After giving birth I was left in the hospital while he got high for two-days. When he finally came to the hospital and took me home, I was beaten, again more viciously than before. Then the verbal abuse started. I was always told, "No one is going to want you; you got two kids. No one will ever want you." I tried so hard to please him and tried to figure out what I was doing to make him hurt me. I made an excuse for everything that he did. He would leave for days on end, coming home with bullet holes in my cars. Thinking back, it is just so unreal that I ever put up with that. He would run in and out of our house taking things to sell or taking money from the house and then he would be gone for days. I had just gotten so used to it that I became numb to everything. His mother came to our house one day to confront him about his drug use, and we convinced him to go to rehab. He went for 30 days and honestly, during that time I was at peace because I was alone. I dreaded his return home because I did not know what new reality I would be faced with. He got out and for about four months, life was normal; there was no fighting, no yelling and I let my guard down. All it took was one night out with the same old crowd and we were back to square one. When he came home that familiar crack smell invaded my bed and I knew my nightmare was about to begin once again.

At the time, I worked in Chicago at a big ten law firm, and I was getting better with my financial stability. Still trying to maintain this fake relationship we were supposed to vacation with family to Florida. The day before the trip he said he could not go because he had mandatory overtime at work. He worked in the Steel Mill and this was not uncommon for them to cancel a vacation, so I went with my two children. Every day that I was gone I called, and he would never answer. I worried, but I was good at masking my emotions by this time. No one ever knew that inside I was in hell. When he dropped me off at the airport, we were in my brand-new van and when he picked me up, he was in his work vehicle. I asked him where my van was and got no answer. We got home and there was no van, so I asked again. The words that escaped his mouth I never thought I would ever hear; he sold my van for an eight ball of crack cocaine! My heart sunk and the only thing I could think of was how I was going to get back and forth to work, and how was I going to transport my kids! The next day I got a ride and bought my own vehicle and would not give him the key. He beat me because my purchase was costing him more money. It did not matter that I had my own job; his only focus was on himself. I began to adapt my life to his drug use and honestly, I made it appear normal. I still left my kids with this man and looking back, I must ask myself- "What the hell was wrong with me?" I think of how things could have gone so wrong because of his addiction and me leaving my kids with him. One night I had to work late, and this man left my four-year-old daughter home alone, sitting on the couch with the tv on, with a bottle and a diaper for her little brother, just so that he could get high. I never left my kids alone with him again and that was the last night I shared my bed with him. The only time there was sexual contact was when he forced himself on me.

I reconnected with one of my childhood friends who was a single mother. Our girls were close in age and honestly, this friend became my angel. I started doing more things with her and it would keep me away from the house even though it never stopped him from beating me. I had my babysitter's teenage daughter who cared for my children, so I could go out with friends and not worry about my kids. He became an object to me because he was binging and messing up his 6-figure job at the steel mill. His absence was my solitude. Then one night I was asleep in my bed; suddenly I was roughly awakened. I looked up into eyes that were crazed, and hate- filled. My husband pulled me out of the bed and dragged me, screaming down the hall and down 13 stairs into the family room. He had dumped my purse out all over the floor. There was a Mary Kay business card with a man's number written on it and he kept yelling that I needed to give him an explanation about that card. I told him that the guy sold Mary Kay, but he didn't believe me, although it was the truth. He beat me repeatedly into the wee hours of the morning. Convinced that he would kill me, I finally told him what he wanted to hear, that the guy was trying to talk to me. He was more enraged by the "lie" that the man sold Mary Kay than he was about a man trying to talk to me. My situation was so bad I called my mother. I was in tears and her response I will never forget… "Call me back when you get done performing, I can't understand you".

Looking back, I realize that she was not aware of the severity of the abuse in my relationship. I never called back, and his response was, "See, I told you no one cares about you". I believed it. This was a precursor to things to come and when I thought it could not get any worse, it did. His drug use grew worse; the binges were lasting weeks on end, and he lost his $100,000 a year steel mill job because he just stopped going. I was driving down the street and the drug dealer was driving my husband's car, so I pulled the guy over. He told me- 'Your old man gave me this car." My husband had even started writing checks to a woman with who he was smoking crack with. He was climbing out of windows in my house just to go get high.

The last straw was when he was on his two-week drug binge and decided to come home. I was up getting dressed for work, the kids were still asleep, and he looked at me and said- "You going to give me some?" I was like- "Hell no. You are a crackhead." That was it! I was slapped and called a lesbian and he did something I never saw coming; he went to the closet pulled out a shotgun and pointed it at my head. He told me I was going to give him what he wanted. My four-year-old daughter woke up and was terrified and went to her brothers' room and took him out of the crib and hid under her bed with him as her father repeatedly raped me for over two hours. I got up trembling and finished getting dressed and I did the unthinkable and left my kids with this man and went to work, I did not know what else to do. I went into my boss's office and collapsed. My best friend was called, she came to pick me up and I called my stepfather in hysterics and said, "I cannot do this no more! Please help me". That was the day that my cry for help was finally answered. I know that had I continued this relationship one or both of us would have been killed. On that day I filed for divorce with my stepfather's help. I had to have a rape exam done. To add insult to injury, I was told that under Indiana law, a husband cannot rape a wife. That was the last day I was his victim but not the last day that I suffered.

By this time, I had met someone and after knowing him for six months, I took another leap of faith and moved to New Jersey to escape the horrible life that I had been living. This was my chance. When it was time for me to go back to Indiana to finalize my divorce, my soon-to-be ex-husband called and threatened to kill me. I was so scared I called my lawyer and just told her- "I do not want a thing. He can have it all!" My lawyer was not having it. I was sick and vomited the entire night. To my surprise, the coward never showed, and the judge gave me everything. It took me years to have a rational conversation with my ex-husband because I hated him so much. As the years progressed, I had to forgive him so I could live.

The life I had with him haunts me every day. I came to tell this story because I felt it was time for me to take this final journey for me to live my life fully. As strange as it sounds, I never told my daughter this story because I never wanted to tarnish her image of her father. There were times that she would scream and cling to me if another man touched me. My life has not been easy, and I suffer daily. I often tell people they should never judge a book by its cover. If I seem a little on edge sometimes, that is my Post Traumatic Stress Disorder (PTSD). If I seem a little sad sometimes, that is my depression. I needed love to heal me. It took me years to realize that the love that I needed was to love myself. My story is still being written.

How Her Story Relates to My Story:

_____

_____

_____

_____

_____

_____

_____

_____

_____

_____

_____

_____

_____

_____

How Her Story Relates to My Story:

_____

_____

_____

_____

_____

_____

_____

_____

_____

_____

_____

_____

_____

Author Tonya Campbell

Tonya Campbell

On the surface, Latonya (Tonya) Campbell is an accomplished Senior Project Manager with a Fortune 500 company and has over twenty-plus years of experience in the financial industry. Tonya is an advocate for change, a survivor on so many levels, and a lover of giving back to the community.

Among the many hats that Tonya wears, her most prized role is that of a mother to two handsome young men, godmother to five young ladies, and partner in a committed long-term relationship. Tonya is a native of De Quincy, Louisiana, where she attended public school and graduated from De Quincy High School in 1991 to pursue her dreams. Born to Barbara Robinson, Tonya is the eldest of four children. She is also a proud Aunt to five nieces and one great nephew.

Tonya earned a Bachelor of Social Work degree in 1995 and is currently continuing her education with Capella University. Throughout her journey in volunteering, Tonya has developed a passionate interest in community involvement with those less fortunate and causes dear to her heart. Tonya has worked very closely with organizations in the local community to support and give back to the homeless population. She never wants anyone to feel that they are forgotten, so she has tried to combat this by showing kindness and love to others. In particular, Tonya has worked very closely with local organizations like: *The Giving Heart, Homeward,* and *The Daily Planet,* to support the homeless population. For many years, prior to the revitalization of Monroe Park, Tonya executed a *Blankets of Blessing* Drive every December to give a gift of warmth, to the homeless, throughout the holiday season. She has also served as the Community Involvement Directress, for the past six years, giving back to those in the Central Virginia area. Tonya worked closely with *Dress for Success,* volunteering her time with events to empower and uplift women. Tonya's desire to assist women battling Breast Cancer led her to supporting the American Cancer Society, for the past fifteen years. Tonya serves in honor of her Aunt Brenda Houston, who succumbed to breast cancer. Tonya spearheaded an event, *It's a Good Hair Day*, to collect new and gently-used wigs and accessories to help the American Cancer Society – Glen Allen Office diversify their wig closet. Tonya's goal was to give women of color viable options, when receiving a wig voucher, to support them on their cancer journey. Tonya's drive to support other breast cancer survivors also connected her with *Here for the Girls*, a non-profit agency improving the lives of young women affected by breast cancer and those diagnosed under the age of 51. With the support of the *Desert of Virginia, Daughters of the Auxiliary of the Ancient Egyptian Arabic Order of the Nobles of the Mystic Shrine of North and South America*, she was able to collect donated items to give a gift of hope, to those undergoing chemotherapy. Tonya knew the challenges that she faced and wanted to pay it forward, by supporting others through their cancer journey. Tonya is currently an active member of the *Here for the Girls*, Richmond Chapter and gained an amazing support team of sisters who can share, understand, and support the breast cancer journey that survivors endure.

Tonya attributes her hard work and community involvement to her mother, who as a single mother, always supported others and exhibited the most selfless act of paying it forward. Tonya lives by the saying, *"God holds you accountable for how you treat people, not how they treat you."* Tonya has spoken on several platforms to share her personal journey, with breast cancer, and wants to encourage others that **you are not alone** and **there are women who support you and champion your success.**

A Journey from Sadness to Survivor

The Three D's: Depressed, Defeated, and in Denial. Yes, that is how 2018 started out for me. I was clearly not in the mood to say "Happy New Year" to anyone because it felt like all the goals I set had already been crushed. What do you do when you are in the prime of your career and are notified that after 17 years with a Fortune 500 company, they will be downsizing, and your name is on the list to be laid off? January 3rd would be my last official day with the company! I wasn't ready for those cards to be dealt to me. I had become very complacently secure with my job and never thought they would select me since I had previously survived three other layoffs.

Reality had kicked in and I was faced with the realization that things, as I had known them, were coming to an end. Now the words I would often share with the participants in a program that I managed would become my own words to myself: *"the most uncomfortable places are truly the places where we grow the most"*. At one point, I thought this was a dream that I had not awakened from. I felt like my whole world was crumbling down like a condemned building that was being demolished. I was suddenly faced with how I would be able to support my household as the sole provider for my children.

Hello, SOMEBODY! I knew major changes had to occur, and I wasn't ready, nor as well prepared as I should have been. I mean, it wasn't like I could call my mom and say to her that I needed to move in with her until I got on my feet, because she didn't live around the corner. She didn't even live in the same city or state. None of my family resided in Richmond except for my two sons and myself; my immediate family was all in Louisiana. I was forced to figure this situation out quickly. At this moment, I was talking to myself in the car, mentally posing so many unanswered questions. How would I be able to afford our lifestyle with minimal changes of comfort that we were used to? I have always strived as a single mother to provide for both of my sons and had started working at the young age of 16. At the time of my layoff, my oldest son was employed at a major brand retail store and was looking at opportunities that would give him advancement, which could result in relocating. Therefore, his main goal was to save money to move if he was selected for a job in another city. I couldn't ask him to contribute and delay or take away from his dreams. My youngest son was a sophomore at Winston Salem State University, a Historically Black University in North Carolina. All I was trying to do was ensure that I didn't disrupt the plans and goals both of my sons had in place for themselves. I was exhausted just thinking about it.

I was sitting at the red light in my car on the corner of Glenside and Broad, - which meant that I was getting closer to my home, but it still felt like I was so many miles away. The only thing at that moment running through my mind was that I needed to get behind closed doors so I could pray. Amid all the chaos that was around me, I never forgot my Church of God in Christ roots, because if I didn't know how to do anything else, I knew how to pray. I knew that God would help me think through my dilemma and make a decision if I trusted him.

I waited until I made it to my bedroom and at that moment so many emotions started to overtake my body. The water swelled up in my eyes and the tears would not stop falling. As they were running slowly down my cheeks, I heard God whisper, "You will be alright!". I realized at that moment that my faith walk was about to be tested. I was struggling between trusting God while fighting with my flesh and trying to step in on something God was working out in his timing and not mine. I was often told by my spiritual mentor that you cannot pray and worry at the same time. Here I go with this self-pep talk, saying to myself, *"Come on girl, get it together. You got this."* It has always been easy for me to encourage others, but at this point, it wasn't easy for me to even encourage myself. Wasn't losing my job enough hardship? Just when I thought that was a lot to manage, I received the biggest blow of my life at the ripe age of 45. I had made several doctors' appointments to prepare myself in the event that I didn't find a full-time job with health benefits. I was trying to ensure that I still had a clean bill of health. Well after being laid off on January 3rd, now on January 16th, I received a call from my doctor that scared me. You must understand, it hits a bit differently when you get a call and it is not the nurse, but the *doctor* who is on the other end of the phone! It was clear this call meant something was not 100% right.

Hello Ms. Campbell. this is Dr. X. I wanted to talk to you about your most recent visit. Are you in a place where you can talk?

With a bit of hesitation, I said, *"Yes, I am...."*

It appears from some of the test results we will need you to come back into the office for some additional tests.

My mind was all over the place but, at this point, I wanted to know what in the world was he really trying to say. I then responded and said, *"Dr. X, I need you to elaborate a little more for me because I don't understand."*

Ms. Campbell, I need you to get to a place where you can take a seat wherever you are, and is anyone there with you?

At this point, my palms were sweating because every thought in my head began to shift to nothing but negative news. I started to feel tingling all over my body and I responded, *"Nobody is here, but I still want to you proceed because I need to know what is going on with my health."*

Dr. X said, *"I am sorry to inform you that you have been diagnosed with Stage 2 Breast Cancer, Invasive Ductal Carcinoma, but we are here to work with you and will provide the best treatment plan for you."*

Those were the only words I heard from him and everything else he was saying sounded like a foreign language that I couldn't understand. It felt like everything paused for a second when he gave me the diagnosis. Then instantly everything around me started to move in slow motion. Before I knew it, the phone disconnected, and I was numb all over. How much more *"kicking me while a person is down"* could any one person take? I never imagined being in the driver's seat of dealing with such a great illness that had no cure.

Breast cancer runs in my family, but I didn't think that it would impact me. My aunt, Brenda, had passed away from breast cancer 14 years' prior, and my sister was faced with having a lumpectomy. My niece had dealt with issues with her breast so I was under the assumption that at my age I wouldn't have to deal with this ugly disease that had impacted my family and friends that I loved dearly. What was I going to do now that my insurance was ending on January 31st? I was walking into this diagnosis with ABSOLUTELY NO INSURANCE! I wouldn't be able to afford COBRA insurance because it was so expensive, and I needed to save my money from my severance package to pay my household bills. Even though I had accepted a contract job, I did not elect to take the insurance because I felt I was in great health, which was clearly not true now, based upon the report from the doctor.

I was not ready to talk to anyone, not even my own family, about what I was experiencing. I felt like a death sentence had been handed to me and I couldn't even utter the "C" word because to me, saying it, felt like I was accepting the diagnosis and I wasn't there yet. KCUF CANCER! How was I supposed to function? Who was going to help me when I only have my sons living in Virginia with me and all my immediate family living 18 hours away? I have always prided myself on being able to help others but now my back was up against the wall because I needed support. One thing I learned over the years in my adult life, is not everyone that states they will help you will actually do it. Many may only say they will help you because it sounds good at the moment during a crisis. I was shielding myself from any let down by people I considered friends. I elected at the time, not to ask for any help, feeling I could resolve things myself.

In February, I received the treatment plan with a lot of fancy words on the paper describing the care to combat the illness. The treatment plan consisted of various milligrams of Herceptin through infusion in 90-minute sessions combined with chemotherapy drugs. With no insurance how would I be able to get the best care? Over the next few months, I received treatment, but it didn't come without a lot of severe side effects and bouts of illness that only a person going through can relate to. With everything around me changing with my health, I did not want anyone to judge me or look at me differently. So, I tried to keep my image up by presenting myself as all put together on the outside. But let me tell you, behind closed doors, I was struggling and battling daily; I was so ready to give up. No one wants to have poison pumped into their body without knowing if it will help you live longer, survive your illness, or if you will succumb to the illness. I had just watched my close friend, Kari, not win the battle against cancer, so my faith was shaken. Then came the bouts of depression, just like I had previously struggled with for so many years. I attended so many therapy sessions and even took prescribed psychotropic drugs to help me sleep and function in moments that presented increased anxiety. I just couldn't bear the pain I was experiencing anymore: physically or mentally. One day in April, I took an overdose of pills to end my life. This was one of many attempts I made to end everything that was occurring in my life. This was a very grim and dark place for me, and my youngest son called 911 because he didn't know what to do to help his mother since he had no clue what I was battling in silence.

Four months and nineteen days was a long time to live in denial about a very ugly disease that had attacked my body. All this time, I had kept it hidden. Although many say I am one of the lucky ones, with an early diagnosis, I was relieved that I didn't have to hide anymore. Unfortunately, soon after my condition was revealed, I wished I had stayed in hiding. I will not group all Black women in one category, A small gesture I thought would implore other women to get annual mammograms turned into me being judged and ridiculed by women who at one time, I respected. I will not group all Black women in one category, but people I considered to be friends, proved themselves to just be associates. All I was trying to do was reach one healthy woman to encourage her to get checked, but I paid a high price for putting my life out on display. Was it worth all the headaches I endured? Everyone's journey with cancer will be different. So even though I share my experience, one must realize it may not be the same for everyone. These people were cruel, and their words truly hurt because so many tried to be the judge, jury, and executioner. I guess it is easier to blame a victim than face the reality that it might happen to you. Cancer can hit anyone at any time and often there is no rhyme or reason for it. What they didn't realize was that my oldest son dealt with caring for me and putting his life on hold to help his mother in a very rough time!

No, what they didn't understand was that I was battling thrash in my mouth which made it hard to eat, constant bouts of nausea, diarrhea more often than I wanted to think of, and laying on the bathroom floor because it was easier to stay close to the toilet when those moments came. I was mentally exhausted. I was rejected by women I tried to help avoid this experience and was left to feel alone and unsupported by "friends".

What many saw on the outside was a woman who seemed strong. What they didn't see was the woman who was so ill, overwhelmed, and depressed that she attempted suicide again. Yes, I ended up having my stomach pumped and responding to a lot of embarrassing questions from the hospital staff. It was at this point that I made an informed decision to protect my energy by only having people in my life who would support me through my journey. Honey let me tell you, having the right support circle is HUGE!!! A dear friend, Aisha Rousseau, whom I love beyond the sky, became my spiritual mentor and would often pray with me, send me text messages, and connected me with a pastor and local mentor to help me through this journey. The biggest supporters outside of my family were two breast cancer survivors and a lady I have admired for over 10 years that provided resources to me. They allowed me to ask them any question and provided honest feedback all the time. They allowed me to talk about my fears and the challenges I was experiencing. They were so supportive. Ruth Ellerbe, Trina Dodson, and Sheila McGlown will forever be my SHEROS; they made a positive impact in my life and I owe them so much. Breast Cancer can happen to you, no matter your age, your race, your gender, or the size of your breasts. God gave me a second chance at life. Everything happens for a reason, so you must live it, love it, and learn from it. I endured 16 rounds of chemotherapy, eight sessions of radiation, a lumpectomy with lymph nodes removed, and I am currently in remission. I grabbed cancer by the bullhorns and fought for my life! I am a mother, daughter, sister, girlfriend, but most of all I AM A SURVIVOR!!

How Her Story Relates to My Story:

_____

_____

_____

_____

_____

_____

_____

_____

_____

_____

_____

_____

_____

Thank you for your support.
~HER STORY Authors

Contact Visionary Michelle Dowleyne At:
Website: *www.michelledowleyne.com*
Email: *AuthorMichelleDowleyne@gmail.com*
Facebook: *Facebook.com/groups/HerStoryIsMyStory/*

shero

publishing

Made in the USA
Middletown, DE
20 March 2021